Eliz

The

MW01199755

Robert Turner has lectured extensively on magic in the
Tudor period for over twenty years. He is a co-author of the
Necronomicon published in 1978, and compiler of
The Heptarchia Mystica of John Dee.

QUEEN ELIZABETH I (attributed to J. Bettes the Younger)
Courtesy of National Portrait Gallery

Elizabethan Magic

The Art and the Magus

Robert Turner

Foreword by
Colin Wilson

With contributory material by
Patricia Shore Turner
and
Robin E. Cousins

Illustrated by
Charles H. Cattell
and
Jane O'Reilly

Translations from the Latin by
Christopher Upton

ELEMENT BOOKS

First published in 1989 by
Element Books Limited
Longmead, Shaftesbury, Dorset

Designed by Jenny Liddle
Cover design by Max Fairbrother

Typeset by Poole Typesetting (Wessex) Limited, Bournemouth
Printed and bound in Great Britain by Billings, Worcester

British Library Cataloguing in Publication Data
Turner, Robert
Elizabethan magic: the art and the magus.
1. England. Occultism, history
I. Title II. Turner, Patricia Shore III. Cousins, Robin E.
133'.0942

ISBN 1-85230-083-3

Contents

*For Desmond H. G. Bourke,
who led me to the true Dee.*

Acknowledgements

My work on the lives and techniques of the Elizabethan Magi began over two decades ago. During this lengthy period I have incurred the debt of the many friends, associates and public bodies who have assisted with my researches. This book is therefore not my achievement alone, but a culmination of the collective efforts of all who have helped to make it possible.

My grateful thanks are due to the British Library Board for granting permission to reproduce material from original Dee manuscripts and the portrait of Simon Forman; to the Wellcome Institute for the engraving from Robert Fludd's *Philosophia Sacra*; to the National Portrait Gallery for the Portrait of Elizabeth I; and the Ashmolean Museum's Department of Western Art for the Portrait of John Dee.

I am greatly indebted to the veteran writer Colin Wilson for taking time out of his hectic schedule to write an admirable Foreword; and to Christian Wilby for the loan of his excellent typescript of Dee's Diaries.

Special thanks to Patricia Shore Turner for her contribution on Twm Sion Cati; Robin E. Cousins for his work on Robert Turner and for compiling the index; Charles Cattell for his excellent artwork; and Christopher Upton for his scholarly Latin translations.

Patricia Shore Turner extends her personal gratitude to M. E. Ling, of Cardiff Central Library for his offer of research facilities; to Christopher Delaney, Curator of Carmarthen Museum for his informative telephone conversation and the photograph of Thomas Jones' claspknife; to Gwynfor Rees of Tregaron Secondary School, for his informative notes, his work at the National Library of Wales, and the high-quality negative of 'The Werna Stones'. To Jane O'Reilly for her impression of Cati and the motif of the swallow-tailed kite; and to the Staff of Wolverhampton Reference Library for their assistance in tracking down various obscure Welsh words.

Robin Cousins wishes especially to thank Bob and Barbara Prichard of Salem, Penrhyncoch, Dyfed for their hospitality and transportation to Ystradffin in order to photograph Twm Sion Cati's Cave; their son Danny Simkins, who knew the concealed location of the cave; and Carol Cousins for long-term encouragement. He also extends his thanks to the British Library Board for permission to reproduce the portrait of Robert Turner and other important items; to the Staff of Hampshire Record Office in Winchester for their assistance during the search for Turner's origins; and to Holy Cross Church, Bearsted for permission to photograph the Fludd Monument in the vestry.

Finally I wish to record my thanks to our Publishers and the staff of Element Books for their indispensable help at every stage of the work; with special thanks to Simon Franklin for his talented editorial work and invaluable guidance.

ROBERT TURNER
December 1988

Foreword

This book is about a number of 'mages' or occultists of the Elizabethan and Stuart era, chief among whom is Dr John Dee. And I foresee that the book is going to cause severe bewilderment among those who expect it only to contain some curious and entertaining sidelights on the history of the sixteenth and seventeenth centuries. This, I suspect, is why I have been asked to write the foreword – to form a bridge between the scholarly authors of this volume and the reader who finds himself growing increasingly confused and exasperated.

The problem is this. Dee, Kelly, Fludd, Simon Forman and the rest took it completely for granted that 'magic' really works, and that it is possible to make contact with angels – or demons – and 'control' them. And we readers of the late twentieth century take it equally for granted that magic is a delusion, a mere historical curiosity. We also take it for granted that the writers of this volume share our enlightened attitude. But the authors offer no clue to their attitude; they prefer to write with scholarly detachment about the strange doings and even stranger ideas of these extraordinary men, and leave us to make up our own minds.

I must confess that I feel this is not an entirely reasonable attitude; so for the benefit of those who share my view, I will do my best to explain why I believe that these half-forgotten mages deserve our sympathetic attention.

Let us begin by admitting that, to the modern intelligence, the story of John Dee is an almost impenetrable mystery. What are we to make of this tale of an Elizabethan scholar – one of the greatest of his age – who experimented with the magical invocation of spirits – while all the time insisting that he was not a magician – and who went on to transcribe a great many books at their dictation? When we learn that Dee's partner in most of these experiments was a dubious young Irishman named Edward Kelly (or Kelley), who had lost both his ears for forgery, it is hard to avoid jumping to the conclusion that Dee was simply the credulous dupe of a confidence trickster. This, for example, is the view taken by Rossell Hope Robbins in his widely circulated *Encyclopedia of Witchcraft and Demonology*, where, after agreeing that Dee was one of the great Elizabethan scholars of 'occult philosophy', he goes on:

Less reputable, possibly, was Dee's connection with John Kelly,

a mountebank with whom, in 1581, at Wootton-in-the-Dale, he
tried to invoke spirits to discover hidden treasure. In spite of his
erudition, or because of it, Dr Dee was easily duped. The most
astounding example of his naïveté was swapping wives with his
assistant Kelly.

Now, as the author of this present volume would quickly point out,
this paragraph contains a remarkable number of inaccuracies. Kelly's
name was Edward, not John. Dee met him in 1582, so could not have
been with him invoking spirits in 1581. In fact, the exploit in question
is supposed to have taken place at Walton-le-Dale (not Wootton-in-
the-Dale) near Lancaster, and Kelly's companion was said to be a man
called Paul Waring, not John Dee. So it would not perhaps be too
unfair to assume that Rossell Hope Robbins does not know what he is
talking about.

But what is the truth – or at least, the 'historical truth' – behind all
this? It is that by the time he was 55 – in 1582 – John Dee was an
enthusiastic searcher for the Philosopher's Stone and the Elixir of
Life, and had frequently attained moods of mystical exaltation. As a
good Christian – and as a student of Paracelsus and Cornelius
Agrippa – he naturally believed in the factual reality of angels or
blessed spirits, and attempted to contact them by gazing into crystals.
According to his diary, he first saw an angel in a crystal globe in May
1581, almost a year before he met Kelly. And in November 1582,
seven months or so after he had met Kelly, Dee was on his knees
praying when a 'sudden glory' filled the west window of his
laboratory, and he saw the angel Uriel. The angel smiled benignly,
and handed Dee a piece of convex crystal, telling him that it would
enable him to communicate with beings of another world and to
foresee the future; then Uriel vanished. So clearly, Dee was not
merely Kelly's dupe. He believed that he had had direct personal
contact with the angel Uriel. And since, whatever else he was, Dee
was no fool, we may take it for granted that Uriel was not Kelly
dressed up in silver paper and sequins.

As to the notion that Kelly was merely a mountebank and
confidence trickster, this is discounted by one of the most dis-
tinguished of modern writers on magic, E. M. Butler, who writes (in
Ritual Magic): 'it could undoubtedly have been one long-drawn-out,
gigantic fraud practised by [Kelly] on Dee . . . Yet I believe that the
generally accepted view of downright and conscious trickery is an
over-simplification which distorts the truth.' (p. 259.)

The truth, she believes, is that Kelly possessed genuine powers of
clairvoyance or crystal-vision, and that he undoubtedly heard and
saw the 'spirits' he described – or firmly believed he did. She goes on

to point out that Kelly was terrified of the 'spirits', believing that they were devils and not angels, and that Kelly had no *need* to keep trying to run away if his only intention was to pull the wool over Dee's eyes. Dee was totally, one-hundred-per-cent, convinced that Kelly was seeing real angels, and there was no need for Kelly to indulge in play-acting. Anyone who has actually gone to the trouble of reading Meric Casaubon's edition of *A True and Faithful Relation of What Passed for Many Yeers Between Dr John Dee and Some Spirits* (1659) – a book of which I happen to possess a modern reprint – will end up, as Dr Butler was, totally convinced that Kelly was no fraud as a clairvoyant. He believed that he saw and heard real spirits.

That, of course, does not mean that he did. It may have been merely a form of self-hypnosis. And this was, in fact, my own view in the days when, in my late teens and early twenties, I first devoured E. M. Butler's *Myth of the Magus, Fortunes of Faust* and *Ritual Magic* (all borrowed from the Wimbledon Public Library). I was quite willing to believe that there may be mysterious unknown forces in the universe; but I could not believe they took the forms of angels and demons. And if I had known the work in those days, I would have thoroughly approved of Lynn Thorndike's classic *History of Magic and Experimental Science*, whose very title informs us that the author regards 'magic' as a crude and confused form of science.

It was when I was asked to write a history of 'the occult' in the late 1960s that I gradually became aware that my view was, to put it mildly, somewhat simplistic. Yet I must emphasise that mine was no sudden and revelatory conversion to 'occultism'. It was, rather, a slow process of understanding of what 'occultism' really means, viewed as a historical phenomenon, and it was in no way opposed to reason and common sense. And perhaps the best way in which I can explain my change of viewpoint is to tell the reader something of what I learnt about the history of 'occultism'.

Our remote ancestors believed in life after death, in the realm of spirits, in clairvoyance and the prophetic power of dreams, in natural magic, and in the mysterious influence of the stars and planets on human destiny. Many of these beliefs were closely bound up with the tenets of the Christian religion. This is why many of the Christian fathers, such as St Augustine, were opposed to the rise of natural science, believing that these attempts to 'put Nature to the question' were blasphemous, and likely to undermine the true faith. The great Roger Bacon was thrown into prison in 1277 for suggesting that man should be prepared to trust the powers of his reason, and probably stayed there until 1292, the year of his death.

But science flourished, with or without the approval of the Church Fathers. And to begin with, there was certainly no conflict between 'magic' and science; Paracelsus was an alchemist as well as a scientist; Kepler was an astrologer as well as an astronomer; even Isaac Newton himself was a practising alchemist. It was not until the 'Age of Reason', the age of Hume and Voltaire, that most intelligent men decided that magic was no more than ignorance and superstition, and turned their backs on it.

Yet it was in the age of Voltaire that 'occultism' received its greatest impetus since the days of Paracelsus and Cornelius Agrippa. A wealthy physician named Anton Mesmer stumbled upon the discovery that some of his patients could be cured of such ailments as stomach cramps by laying a powerful magnet on their stomachs. And when he was bleeding a patient, he noticed that the flow of blood increased when he brought a magnet close, and diminished when he took it away. That meant that the human body must possess its own form of magnetism – Animal Magnetism, so to speak. Mesmer convinced himself that if magnets were immersed in water, the water became 'magnetised', and could effect cures. Even trees and grass could be magnetised, so that patients who lay in the garden could receive the benefit.

We are inclined to believe that Mesmer had merely discovered the power of 'suggestion'. Yet we could be oversimplifying. For example, in the 1870s, doctors in the asylum at Rochefort began a series of experiments on a youth named Louis Vivé, who was suffering from hysterical paralysis of the right side of his body after being bitten by a viper; they discovered that the paralysis could be transferred from his right to his left side if he was stroked with steel; but nothing happened if they tried other metals. And thirty years earlier, Baron Karl von Reichenbach had also discovered that magnets could produce a powerful effect on his own patients, and he went to some trouble to make sure that this was not merely a matter of suggestion – for example, getting an assistant to hold a powerful magnet on the other side of the wall from the patient's bed, whereupon she instantly detected its presence.

Mesmer was soon branded a charlatan by his fellow doctors, and driven out of Vienna. Yet many doctors were more open-minded (and less envious) than their Viennese colleagues, and came to acknowledge that animal magnetism is not simply a matter of auto-suggestion. One of these was Dr Joseph Ennemoser, who held the Chair of Medicine at the University of Bonn from 1819, and whose massive *History of Magic* still deserves to be read as a fascinating introduction to the subject. Ennemoser believed that 'magnetism' is one of the basic unrecognised principles of life, and that it permeates all nature. But he also concluded that 'a certain prophetic faculty is a common property of the human race, which becomes conspicuous in proportion as man withdraws himself from the external physical world', and that this 'withdrawal' into himself enables man to discover a 'higher power of the spirit'.

Ennemoser's book fascinated a man of letters named William Howitt, and in 1852, during a voyage to Australia, he settled down to translating the work into English. While on this voyage, he had a dream experience that seemed to confirm Ennemoser's views. He dreamed of being at his brother's house in Melbourne, and observed it in detail: a wood of eucalyptus trees, greenhouses by a wall, and a sloping hillside. On his arrival in Australia, he and his two sons walked along until Howitt recognised the wood of his dreams, and told his sons that they would shortly see his brother's house. A moment later, it came into view, exactly as he had seen it in his dream.

In the following year, his wife – back in England – had a dream in which she received a letter from her son saying 'My father is very ill.' She woke up deeply disturbed. She wrote to her husband the next day describing the dream. Six days later she received a letter telling her that her husband had been very ill, but was now better.

Sceptics will have no difficulty demolishing both these examples, pointing out that we only have Howitt's word for it that the scenery was 'identical', and that Mrs Howitt's dream was probably coincidence. But Howitt went to the trouble of collecting a 150-page appendix to his translation of Ennemoser, with dozens of other examples of 'paranormal phenomena'. A few years earlier, a novelist named Catherine Crowe had assembled a similar collection of anecdotes of the paranormal, and her book *The Night Side of Nature* (1848) became a well-deserved bestseller. But it was not until thirty-four years later, with the foundation of the Society of Psychical Research, that meticulous collection of evidence made it clear that, whatever Voltaire and Hume had to say to the contrary, paranormal phenomena were a reality of human experience and not a product of human credulity.

Now many of these phenomena investigated by the Society for Psychical Research would now be labelled 'paranormal powers of the unconscious mind'; they included telepathy, clairvoyance, premonitions, and the peculiar phenomena known as doppelgangers or 'phantasms of the living'. But the Society's researches also made it perfectly clear that there was just as much solid evidence for the existence of ghosts and 'poltergeists' – or 'banging ghosts'. And although some of this evidence might be explained away in terms of telepathy or 'clairvoyance', some of it seemed to indicate quite unequivocally that human beings survive their bodily death.

In fact, new and startling evidence for 'survival' had burst upon the world in the year Mrs Crowe's *Night Side of Nature* appeared. As every student of the paranormal knows, 1848 was the year when a series of extraordinary phenomena began in the house of the Fox family in Hydesville, New York. Mrs Fox asked the neighbours in to hear the loud rapping noises that were keeping the family awake. An exceptionally bold neighbour asked aloud whether the entity was a 'spirit', and a single loud rap answered in the affirmative. The 'spirit' claimed to be the ghost of a peddler who had been murdered in the house by the previous tenant. Now if this had been proved, and the previous tenant hanged, it would have caused a worldwide sensation, and convinced most people of the reality of 'spirits'. What actually happened was that the accused man indignantly protested his innocence, excavations in the cellar failed to reveal the corpse, and it was not until more than half a century later that a skeleton and a peddler's box were discovered accidentally when a wall collapsed in the cellar.

At all events, the poltergeist phenomena in the Fox household led to the foundation of the Spiritualist Church, and within a couple of years, America was full of 'mediums' who summoned up spirits. Scientists reacted with outrage to this new outbreak of 'superstition' – and of course, there can be no doubt that many of these mediums *were* fraudulent. But anyone who takes the trouble to study the evidence will end up totally convinced that many of them – probably the majority – were genuine.

In my book *Afterlife* I have jocularly labelled these events 'the invasion of the spirit people'. Which raises the interesting question: why did 'spirits' (if that is what they were) wait until 1848 to begin manifesting themselves *en masse*? The answer is almost certainly that they didn't. Edward Kelly was practising 'mediumship' more than two centuries earlier, and so were most of the 'magicians' and necromancers from the Witch of Endor to Simon Forman and Robert Fludd. 'Psychics' (as we now call them) have always existed, and the chief characteristic of a psychic is that he or she can see things that other people cannot see.

So what happened in the nineteenth century was not the discovery of the paranormal, but the rediscovery. Of course, the new materialistic science fought it every inch of the way. Auguste Comte declared that human history had passed through three stages: the theological stage, when man invented the gods to try to explain the mysteries of nature, the metaphysical stage, when his intellect begins to overthrow the gods but sets up more subtle 'metaphysical' superstitions in their place, and the positive or scientific, when all the superstitions would vanish like spectres at cockcrow, and man would achieve certainty in the calm light of reason. Comte and his followers – who included most of the scientists of the nineteenth century – were quite certain that all 'occultism' could be dismissed as superstition. We, of course, can see clearly that they had simply thrown out the baby with the bathwater.

Yet a few men of science, like Ennemoser, found themselves unable to concur with this simplistic view; they knew that the evidence for the paranormal is overwhelming. Mesmer's disciple the Marquis de Puységur had also made a discovery of immense importance – hypnosis. He had accidentally placed a shepherd named Victor Race in a trance, and found that in this state he could answer questions and carry out orders just as if wide awake. But Puységur also discovered that Victor Race could read his thoughts while hypnotised, and would obey orders that were not spoken aloud, but given mentally. Again, the medical profession simply declined to accept this observation – in fact, the medical profession continued to regard hypnosis as a delusion for most of the nineteenth century. In the 1840s, a young schoolteacher named Alfred Russel Wallace – co-founder of the theory of evolution by natural selection – tried hypnotising some of his pupils, and was amazed to discover that some of them *could* read his mind; when one of these was in a trance he could share Wallace's sense of taste and smell – he grimaced if Wallace tasted salt and smiled if he tasted sugar – and would wince and rub the appropriate part of his body if Wallace stuck a pin in himself. It was these experiments that eventually led Wallace to suggest the founding of a society for investigating paranormal phenomena, a body that eventually became the Society for Psychical Research.

Now when I began to study the 'paranormal' in the late 1960s, in order to write a commissioned book about it, I was quite prepared to discover that most of it was pure delusion and wishful thinking. But it was only a matter of weeks before I realised that such a view would simply not hold water. My original theory of the paranormal was that man possesses all kinds of hidden abilities – such as telepathy and a 'sixth sense' of danger – which civilisation has suppressed, or allowed to drift into disuse. I was inclined to believe that such phenomena as ghosts and poltergeists are simply manifestations of this 'unconscious' part of the mind. This was the view that I expressed in *The Occult* (1971) and its sequel *Mysteries* (1978). And I must admit that I was deeply disturbed when, in the early 1980s, I was asked to write a book on poltergeists and reached the conclusion that they are, in fact, 'spirits'. But I still firmly believe that it is so. I do not regard myself as a 'spiritualist', I am not particularly interested in the subject of 'survival', and I am not really all *that* deeply interested in 'the occult' as such. Yet I have to acknowledge that twenty years' study of the subject has left me in no doubt whatever that 'spirits' exist, and that the evidence for life-after-death is very powerful indeed.

One more observation, and I shall be ready to return to John Dee and the other subjects of this book. It was Guy Lyon Playfair, the author of *The Flying Cow*, a study of 'voodoo' in Brazil – where he spent many years – who made me aware that there is a close connection between 'magic' and 'spirits'. I had been willing to accept the reality of both black and white magic, but had been inclined to explain them in terms of the 'unknown' powers of the human mind. But Playfair had seen 'black magic' in operation in Brazil, and had evidence to indicate that the 'spirits' involved are the same entities that in Europe we call poltergeists. The *umbanda* magician summons them with certain elaborate and precise rituals – the 'spirits' are sticklers for precision – and persuades them to carry out his will. Max Freedom Long had observed the same thing in Hawaii at the turn of the century, and describes it all in a remarkable book called *The Secret Science Behind Miracles* – an off-putting title for a truly extraordinary piece of work.

When the writer Richard Deacon decided to write a book about John Dee, he consulted the historian Hugh Trevor-Roper. And Trevor-Roper made the following interesting comments:

> You have chosen a *very* difficult subject, and I wonder if you realise how difficult it is. The biographical side of Dee is no doubt straightforward. But to *understand* his work (largely misunderstood by those who wrote about him) . . . one has to learn a new language to interpret the 'natural magicians' of the pre-Baconian world.

Now since Trevor-Roper is the author of a book called *The European Witch-Craze in the Sixteenth and Seventeenth Centuries*, we may take it that he does not have the slightest belief in the reality of 'magic' or the paranormal. At the same time, he is too intelligent a man to dismiss Dee as an utterly deluded old man. In some obscure way, he realises that these strange works taken down at the dictation of 'angels' are not mere gobbledegook, but that they require a completely different attitude of mind from that of our post-Baconian era to understand them. If we can go this far with Professor Trevor-Roper, then we shall at least be prepared to understand why Robert Turner is willing to devote so much effort to the study of texts that will strike most of us as totally meaningless.

I, of course, am prepared to venture at least one stage further. A few years ago, I was deeply impressed by a book on the Swedish mystic Emanuel Swedenborg by an American psychiatrist called Wilson Van Dusen. Dusen had been the chief medical officer in the state mental institution at Mendocino, California, and had made the interesting observation that there was a strange similarity between the delusions of patients who were haunted by 'voices'. Most of the 'spirits' seen by his patients seemed to be of a low order; like stupid and naughty children, they would jeer, sneer and repeat silly catch-phrases over and over again. But there was another type of 'spirit' that seemed to belong to an altogether higher order; these were intelligent and sympathetic, and seemed bent on helping the patient. Through his patients, Van Dusen was able to engage in dialogues with these 'spirits' – exactly as Dee engaged in dialogues with 'angels' through Kelly. He also observed that they seemed to correspond very closely to two types of 'spirit' described by Swedenborg – 'high' or 'low' (that is, angelic or diabolic) spirits. The 'low' spirits also seem to correspond to the mischievous spirits evoked by Brazilian *umbanda* specialists.

I would suggest, then, that once we begin to understand a little of the history of 'magic' and 'occultism', we shall begin to take a new look at figures like Simon Forman, John Dee and Robert Fludd. Even the much-despised science of astrology, as practised by Dee and Forman, may prove to be of far greater significance than we suppose, if the views of scientists like Michel Gauquelin, H. J. Eysenck and Dr Percy Seymour prove to have any foundation in fact.

Finally, let me advise you to take a close look at Simon Forman's account of his encounter with a 'spirit' on page 94, and Robert Fludd's description of his own use of 'geomantic astrology' to assess the character of a young girl (p. 103 *et seq.*). We may, admittedly, decide to doubt Fludd's word about the accuracy of his assessment, since the anecdote occurs in the introduction to one of his own books. But why should Forman bother to write such an account in his private diary – meant only for his own eyes – if he was lying? Such questions as this struck me many times as I read the typescript of this book, and left me with an increasingly strong feeling that what is being described is not some kind of delusion, but simply an order of reality with which I am personally unacquainted. I do not possess the key to many of the mysteries in this book, and I am inclined to doubt whether anyone in the twentieth century is qualified to understand them completely. But even without the advice of Professor Trevor-Roper, I would be prepared to believe that there is a great deal here that deserves the most careful and sympathetic study.

COLIN WILSON
Gorran Haven
Cornwall, 1988

Introduction

This book is intended to be read on two interrelated levels. Firstly, it represents the crystallisation of over twenty years of research into Elizabethan magical practice, incorporating several highly important theurgic tracts together with extensive commentaries, analytical notes and textual annotations. Secondly, in order to invigorate the general content of the work and banish the gloomy spectre of dull academic presentation, we provide a necessary insight into the personalities of the colourful and multi-talented Masters of these curious Arts. These inclusions have not been injected purely for biographical reasons, but rather in the hope that our efforts towards furnishing a better understanding of these men and their times will lend credence and authority to the work of the Elizabethan Magus.

My first attempt towards unravelling the mysteries of Elizabethan magic are recorded in my work *The Heptarchia Mystica of John Dee*,[1] which sets forth a system of planetary Invocations hitherto unparalleled in the history of occultism. The present book can be seen as an amplification of this primary volume, yet, pursuing the matter to a much greater depth, contrasting Dee's more advanced techniques with those of his contemporaries. Here the reader will find John Dee's three major magical texts set out in their entirety, which coupled with what has already been accomplished in *The Heptarchia* represent the sum total of magical manuscripts emanating from this source.

At this point I feel it necessary to digress from the general theme of this introduction in order to tender my views upon what has been recently written on the present subject, with particular reference to the so-called *Enochian System*.

First and foremost amongst four books that have come to my attention is a work entitled *The Enochian Evocation of Dr John Dee*, edited and translated by Geoffrey James.[2] This volume purports to be an accurate rendering of the four important digests of Dee's 'Spiritual Diaries' contained in the British Library Sloane collection.[3] Unfortunately, Geoffrey James's book is from the outset marred by elements of pure speculation and, more seriously, suffers greatly from highly inadequate and inaccurate Latin translations. An example of James at his worst serves to illustrate my point:

(James's translation of the final marginal note in John Dee's *De Heptarchia Mystica*)

See also the sayings of Ephodius where, concerning Adamanta, in which diverse signs are given for responding to God. See Epiphanius concerning precious stones and their meaning. See his writings concerning the Unim[4] and Thummim. See the book received at Trebonae. It is written in the books of Epiphanius that the vision that appeared to Moses on the mountain, the laws that were given were expressed in sapphires.[5]

(cf. Christopher Upton's translation of the above passage taken from my edition of *The Heptarchia Mystica*[6])

See Suidas on the word Ephod [where he writes of] the diamond in which, on giving of various signs, the answers from God proceeded.
See Epiphanius with the same argument on precious stones.
See the Scriptures on Urim and Thummim.
See the books received at Trebona.
It is written in the law [says Epiphanius] that the vision which appeared to Moses on the Mount and the law given was expressed in a sapphire, or the Memorabilium of Mizaldus, cent. 4, no. 94.[7]

When one compares the above translation with that given by James it is immediately evident that the American version is seriously in error. We see the word *Ephod*[8] – an ornamental girdle worn by the Hebrew priests – rendered as a proper noun 'Ephodius'; omissions, contractions and inversions abound – together with the frequent interchange of plural for singular. In short, this misleading translation adds considerable confusion to an inherently complex subject.

Furthermore, as Geoffrey James omits any example of Dee's Latin, the scholarly reader is denied the opportunity of judging for himself.

It will be seen that in the present volume, and all that I have written previously regarding these matters, samples of the original Latin have been included to avoid these defects.

Finally, one can only wonder at the use of the word *Evocation* in the title of James's book, a term widely associated with demonology and the necromantic arts, rather than the angelically orientated word *Invocation*.

Curiosity prompted my recent purchase of two books (expensive paperbacks) by Gerald Schueler: *Enochian Magic – A Practical Manual*, and its sequel: *An Advanced Guide to Enochian Magick*.[9] With cover captions declaring 'The Angelic Language Revealed', 'A Complete Manual of Angelic Magic', we are led to expect something rather more than an unsavoury mixture of the highly synthetic techniques of the Golden Dawn and Aleister Crowley's Astrum Argentinum.

To add to the overall confusion of this text the author sees fit to introduce elements of Eastern mysticism; sex magic; the Whore of Babylon; and directions for the ritual use of cupcakes – yes, cupcakes![10]

In the introductory passages of Schueler's text John Dee is referred to as 'Sir'[11] (he was never knighted) and we are informed of how Edward Kelly 'robbed Dee of what little money he had left, helped Dee's wife to pack her bags [and, with her] left Dee never to return': a fact history fails to record. (Dee's third wife Jane remained with him throughout her life. She died of plague in 1605. Kelly met his death during 1595.)

In other sections of Schueler's books we are introduced to the 'Ninety-two Governors' of the Aethers; all other sources, including Crowley, give ninety-one.[12] And, in addition, a Tarot deck of seventy-two Keys rather than the traditional seventy-eight.

To list the errors and misconceptions contained in this lamentable volume would be both tedious and unnecessary. To the intelligent and informed reader they will appear only too obvious; for those embarking on such studies for the first time, a perilous pitfall.

It is hoped that the above comments will serve their purpose in guiding the reader towards a more accurate understanding of John Dee's Angelic Magic, and to some measure, prevent his enraged spirit from wreaking vengeance on his literary assassins.

In contrast to the mediocrity of the works so far encountered, Gerald Suster's book *John Dee Essential Readings*[13] can be recommended as a scholarly and erudite representation of a number of important tracts written between 1556 and the beginning of the seventeenth century. Apart from the author's over-reliance on the magical experiments of Aleister Crowley[14] and the Golden Dawn, I have only one criticism of his digest. This concerns a factual error which occurs in Chapter 8, where an item which claims to have been taken from Dee's *Liber Logaeth* (Sloane MS. 3189) in fact proves to be an extract from *Liber Mysteriorum Quinti Appendix* (the Appendix to Dee's Fifth Book of the Mysteries – Sloane MS. 3188). The entry is for Sunday, 8 May 1583 and marked by a crude marginal sketch of a headsman's axe. It is as follows:

Dee: As concerning the Vision which yesternight was presented (unlooked for) to the sight of EK as he sat a supper with me, in my hall, I meane the appearing of the very sea, and many ships thereon, and the cutting of the hed of a woman, by a tall blak man, what we are to imagin thereof?

Ur[iel]: The one did signifie the provisions of forrayn powers against the welfare of this land: which they shortly put into practice. The other, the death of the Queene of Scotts. It is not long unto it.

The *Liber Logaeth* – apart from a single flyleaf note and a few minor marginal items – contains not a vestige of text, being comprised solely of a series of elaborate alphabetic and numerical squares.[15]

Returning to the present work, I must emphasise that in all instances we have been at pains to ensure that each element of the text has received our in-depth attention. Placing our reliance on original sources, records and official documents, we have done our utmost to avoid the errors perpetuated in former works of this nature. Where translations from the Latin have proved necessary, they have been executed with special care to provide an accurate and intelligible rendering. In addition, for the benefit of classical scholars wishing to make their own comparisons, we have appended examples of the original and unadulterated texts in each instance.

In preparing the typescript upon which the core of this book is based, I have utilised the following manuscripts:

> *Libri Mysteriorum*, Books I–V (1581–1583)
> *Liber Mysteriorum Sextus et Sanctus* (1583)
> *Libri Mysteriorum*, Books VII – XVIII (1583–1587)
> *48 Claves Angelicae* (1584)
> *Liber Scientiae, Auxilii et Victoriae Terrestris* (1585)[16]
> *A Book of Supplications and Invocations* (date unknown)

I have also made use of Elias Ashmole's transcriptions and notes on the above,[17] and Meric Casaubon's printed version of John Dee's Spiritual Diaries VII–XVIII.[18] Other documents, printed works and spurious manuscripts referred to during textual preparation will be found annexed to the relevant sections.

The same care which has been devoted to the textual information presented in this volume is also extended to the artwork. Whenever possible we have reproduced diagrams and engravings in facsimile; where we have been unable to employ original material due to a particular manuscript's poor state of preservation or general illegibility, items have been redrawn from source-works and treble-checked for accuracy. Illustrations from spurious texts not specifically intrinsic to – but relevant by way of explanation of – complete manuscripts, can be found in: Appendix B.

As I have mentioned earlier in this Introduction, much of the material contained in this book can be seen as an extension of the preliminary ideas set forth in my *Heptarchia Mystica*. Where the major theme of the Heptarchial text can be unerringly designated Planetary in nature (The Sevenfold Kingdom), the later Dee manuscripts that form the bulk of the present work can, with equal certainty, be regarded as Elemental. This statement, which some 'authorities' may deem to be at variance with certain established traditions, I defend unreservedly in the commentaries I have supplied in section III.

Since the turn of the century occultists have attached tremendous importance to the aspect of Dee's Angel Magic known as Enochian (after the biblical Enoch), in some instances with little justification. The essence of this 'system' centres on the existence of forty-eight Keys[19] (or Calls) written in what is claimed to be the language of the Angels (a laborious account regarding the reception of these tongue-twisting ejaculations can be found in the Dee manuscripts which emerged between 1583 and 1584).

The clairvoyant abilities of Edward Kelly (Dee's scryer and assistant) form the rock on which these strange Apocalyptic communications stand. In a manner which – due to lack of information – is little understood, Kelly transmitted verbally, or indicated by some other method, each word of the Invocations (in most cases) letter by letter backwards. Kelly's visions were granted while sitting or kneeling at a specially constructed table, known as the 'Holy Table' or 'Table of Practice'[20] and gazing intently into the shew stone (one of Dee's various crystals).

English translations of the forty-eight Keys were obtained by a similar process and set down in a manner that facilitates direct comparison between the Angelic language and our own tongue. An example extracted from Dee's spiritual 'action' recorded at Cracovia (Poland) on Thursday 12 July 1584 serves to illustrate the systematic method he used to tabulate these Invocations:

Angelic	English	Pronunciation
MADRIAX	O you heavens	Madriax
DSPRAF	which dwell	Ds praf
LIL	In the first air	Lil
CHISMICAOLZ	are mighty	Chis Micāolz
SAANIR	in the parts	Sa ā nir
CAOSGO	of the earth	Ca ōs go
OD	and	Od
FISIS	execute	Fisis
BALZIZRAS	the judgement	Balzizras
IAIDA	of the highest	Ia -ida[21]

These lofty and sophisticated utterances seem far removed from the somewhat crude and archaic ritual of Dee's Heptarchial 'grimoire', but nevertheless owe their very existence to this primal and embryonic work:

O noble Prince (N) and by what name else soever thou art called, or mayst truly and duly be called: to whose peculiar Government, Charge and Disposition, Office and Princely Dignity doth appertain thee (N etc.)

In the name of Almighty God, the King of Kings, and for his honour and Glory to be advanced to my faithful service. I require thee, O Noble Prince (N) to come presently, and to show thyself to my perfect and sensible eye judgement, with thy Ministers servants and subjects, to my comfort and help, in Wisdom and Power according to the properties of thy noble office:

COME, O Noble Prince (N) I say, COME, Amen. Pater noster, etc.[22]

The *Enochian* (or Angelic) language has been the subject of considerable discussion (and conjecture) over the past few decades. Scholars of various academic standings have hotly debated whether the transmitted text represents a valid tongue, a cipher, or is merely elaborate gibberish invented by Edward Kelly. Most important amongst various offerings that have come to print in recent times is *The Complete Enochian Dictionary* by Dr Donald C. Laycock.[23] This laudable work can at once be seen to be an honest and erudite attempt to solve some of the mysteries surrounding Dee's Enochian. Laycock sets out his case in full: approaching each element of the problem with methodical care he establishes several important points, not the least of which is the English-like nature of the 'language'. He also aptly dismisses the possibility of Dee's magic being a complex cover for a system of encipherment – I have written elsewhere of my own inclination towards this point of view.[24]

Yet, as one might have expected from the statement which Laycock makes in his second paragraph: 'strangest of all is that we still do not know whether it is a natural language or an invented language – or whether it is, perhaps, the language of the angels,'[25] and despite his employment of computer analysis and other sophisticated techniques, the matter remains largely unsolved and inconclusive.

Finally, while not wishing to detract from the overall value of Dr Laycock's otherwise highly commendable work, a number of textual errors and inconsistencies were noted.[26]

With regard to the pronunciation of individual Angelic words, the only real guide on which one can rely with any degree of certainty is that contained within Dee's own notes on the subject. Several alternative methods of vocalising the Calls have been generated in modern times, the best-known examples emanating from the Hermetic Order of the Golden Dawn via the prolific – if overcomplicated – pen of MacGregor Mathers (1854–1918), and the work of Aleister Crowley.

The Golden Dawn method – from which Crowley's version is directly derived – entails the insertion of the next following Hebrew vowel between each consonant of a given Enochian word; therefore, treating each letter of each word separately. Thus: E after B (bEth), I after G (gImel), A after D (dAleth), and so forth. This highly synthetic manner of dealing with Enochian words is inconsistent, cumbersome, and above all, far removed from the magic of Dee and Kelly.[27]

Before moving on to the final section of this introduction, I feel it would be appropriate to make mention of certain spurious Angelic names that have been added to the Enochian Hierarchy by later commentators.

Foremost amongst these often meaningless constructions are the 'Three Names of God Almighty coming forth from The Thirty Aethers':

1. LAZodaPeLameDaZodaZODaZodILaZodUOLaTaZoda PeKALaTaNuVaDaZodaBeReTa.
2. IROAIAEIIAKOITaXEAEOHeSIOIITEAAIE.
3. LaNuNuZodaTaZodODaPeXaHEMAOANuNuPeRePe NuRAISAGIXa.

These names certainly do not originate with Dee and, although the pronunciation pattern is pure Golden Dawn, the only reference that I have been able to find regarding these fabrications is in *The Equinox*, Vol. 1, No. 8. I therefore conclude that the names were an invention of Aleister Crowley, or a member of his Order.

The method by which these 'names' were constructed will be immediately obvious to anyone familiar with the sequence of the Thirty Aires or Aethers set down by Dee and Kelly.

It is only necessary to write the title of each Aether in their naturally occurring order – from LIL to TEX – one beneath the other, and read down each column adding the relevant Hebrew vowels as required.

At the risk of proving tedious to the informed reader, but in an effort to elucidate upon the matter for those embarking on these studies for the first time, I tender the graphic explanation given on page 8.

Four further names can be found in both the papers of the Golden Dawn and the *Equinox* publications of Aleister Crowley. They are held to be the titles of the 'Four Supreme Elemental Kings'. For reasons best known to himself, Dr Laycock ascribes the origination of these names to Dee – despite the fact that no extant manuscript of the *Libri Mysteriorum* series or any of the condensations recorded in Sloane MS. 3191 make mention of these.

The Three Names of God Almighty
coming forth from The Thirty Aethers:

Name:	(1)	(2)	(3)	
	L	I	L	(1st)
	A	R	N	
	Z	O	M	
	P	A	Z	
	L	I	T	
	M	A	Z	
	D	E	O	
	Z	I	D	
	Z	I	P	
	Z	A	X	
(a) For each God name read	I	C	H	
downwards as indicated: ↓	L	O	E	
	Z	I	M	
	V	T	A	
	O	X	O	↓
(b) For the names of the Thirty	L	E	A	
Aethers read horizontally: LIL,	T	A	N	
ARN, ZOM, etc.	Z	E	N	
	P	O	P	
	C	H	R	
(c) Hebrew vowels to be	A	S	P	
inserted where required. Z to be	L	I	N	
rendered as : Zod (Golden Dawn	T	O	R	
rule).	N	I	A	
	V	T	I	
	D	E	S	
	Z	A	A	
	B	A	G	
	R	I	I	
	T	E	X	(30th)

For the truth of the matter we need look no further than the Golden Dawn paper entitled *Document X, The Book of the Concourse of the Forces*.[28] Here we find full instructions regarding the formation of these names: TAHAOELOG (Air), THAHEBYOBEAATANUM (Water), THAHAAOTAHE (Earth), and OHOOOHAATON (Fire).[29]

The method employed to generate the above names is based entirely on the manipulation of the letters and numbers contained in the outer circle of John Dee's Principal Seal: SIGILLUM DEI AEMETH (The Sign of Truth, the Name of God).[30] Even so, Mathers had to resort to some highly questionable manoeuvres and distortions of the Dee/Kelly system to arrive at these uncalled-for additions.

In my treatment of the three major Dee manuscripts (*48 Claves Angelicae, Liber Scientiae Auxilii et Victoriae Terrestris*, and *A Book of Supplications and Invocations*), I have adopted the following approach:

1. A short discourse on the life of John Dee, together with an account of the circumstances and procedures leading to the construction of these texts.
2. A presentation of the above manuscripts in their entirety with translations from the Latin where applicable.
3. Commentaries on each manuscript.

In addition I have appended a series of explanatory diagrams, an expansion of Dee's *Liber Scientiae Auxilii et Victoriae Terrestris* (for which I am indebted to the scholarship of Robin E. Cousins and the fine artwork of Charles Cattell), an account of *Liber Logaeth*, and an example of the Latin text of *A Booke of Supplications and Invocations*. These offerings, together with what has already been published in my *Heptarchia Mystica*, represent the entire range of John Dee's accessible magical writings that have come down to us.

At the beginning of this Introduction I made mention of the binary nature of the ensuing work. To accomplish this end we have annexed a series of 'brief lives', in an attempt to present manuscript material in context, and to provide some account of the prevailing intellectual and social climate of the Tudor era.

In an effort to avoid needless repetition of what can already be found in print, we have whenever possible directed our attention towards lesser-known, or in many cases hitherto unknown, episodes in the lives of our subjects. Here you will find biographical details regarding John Dee's principal seer Edward Kelly; the enigmatic Dr Simon Forman; the sophisticated Rosicrucian and Kabbalistic thinker Robert Fludd; Dee's elusive Welsh cousin Thomas Jones (alias Twm Sion Cati); and not least the much quoted, yet little understood, Robert Turner of Holshott.

Much of the above information is presented for the first time in print, especially with regard to Patricia Shore Turner's work on *Thomas Jones of Tregaron*, and Robin E. Cousins' detailed analysis of Turner's life and literary achievements. In both instances the authors have provided the reader with painstaking digests of all extant material, and in so doing, bridge several long-neglected historical chasms.

It is hoped that these inclusions will prove of absorbing interest to those who wish to form an overall picture of these fascinating times, so necessary towards a complete and in-depth understanding of Elizabethan magic.

ROBERT TURNER
Wolverhampton, 1988

Notes

1   *The Heptarchia Mystica of John Dee*, ed. Robert Turner, Aquarian Press, 1986.
2   *The Enochian Evocation of Dr John Dee*, ed. and tr. Geoffrey James, Heptangle Books, New Jersey, 1984.
3   Sloane MS. 3191.
4   This word should read Urim, possibly a typographical error.
5   *The Enochian Evocation of Dr John Dee*, p. 64n.
6   *The Heptarchia Mystica of John Dee*, Aquarian Press, 1986, p. 71.
7   Ibid., Lat. '*Vide suidam in dictione Ephod. Ubi de Adamante quo diversis datis signis responsa deo consequebatur. Vide: Epiphanium de Lapidibus praetiosis Rationali isto. Vide Scripturas de Urim et Thummim. Vide Libros receptos Trebonae, etc. Scriptum est in Lege (inquit Epiphanius) Visionem quae Mosi in Monte apparuit et Legem datam in gemma Sapphyro fuisse expressam. Aut Mizaldus Memorabilium, centuria 4, numero 94.*'
8   The word *Ephod* is derived from *aphad*, to tie, to fasten, to gird. In use the girdle passed in various ways across the body of the High Priest and finally over the shoulders with the ends hanging to the ground. Where the Ephod passed over the shoulders were attached two large precious stones, on which the names of the twelve Tribes of Israel were engraved, six on each. When David, Saul, or Joshua wished to consult with God they employed the mysterious Urim and Thummim (perhaps black and white stones), but if they failed to obtain an answer they turned to the High Priest in order to invoke the oracular powers of the Ephod. 'Saul inquired of the Lord,' and that, 'the Lord answered him not, neither by dreams, nor by Urim, nor by prophets.' . . . consequently (on the direction of the Urim) he put on the Ephod (I Sam. 28:6).
See *Calmet's Dictionary of the Holy Bible*, Charles Taylor, London, 1845, pp. 381–2.
Manly P. Hall also ascribes similar powers to the Ephod: 'when the High Priest asked certain questions, they (the stones of the Ephod) emitted a celestial radiance. When the onyx on the right shoulder was illuminated it signified that Jehovah answered the question of the High Priest in the affirmative, and when the left one gleamed, it indicated a negative answer to the query.' (*The Secret Teachings of all Ages*, Manly P. Hall, California, 1962.)
9   *Enochian Magic – A Practical Manual* and *An Advanced Guide to Enochian Magick*, Gerald J. Schueler, Llewellyn Publications, Minnesota, 1987.
10   *An Advanced Guide to Enochian Magick*: G. J. Schueler, pp. 151, 153, 155, 157, etc.

11   Ibid., p. 1.

12   The term 'Governors' used in this context seems peculiar when one considers Dee's Latin title for the column of these ninety-one names given in *Liber Scientiae Auxilii et Victoriae Terrestris* (his work on the thirty Aethers or Aires, 'The Book of Earthly Science, of Help, and of Victory'):

'91 Partium Terra Nomina Divinitus imposita'

(*91 Names of the Parts of the Earth divinely given*. Sloane MS. 3191).

The form utilised by Schueler seems to have originated with Crowley – see *The Equinox* Vols. 7 and 8 – who probably never saw Dee's original manuscript and relied on Casaubon's printed version to be found in *A True and Faithful Relation of What passed for many Yeers Between Dr John Dee . . . and Some Spirits*, ed. Meric Casaubon, London, 1659.

13   *John Dee Essential Readings*, selected and introduced by Gerald Suster, Crucible Press, 1986.

14   Ibid., p. 143. Here Mr Suster treats us to a lengthy extract from Crowley's *The Vision and the Voice*, which shows the Thelemite brushmarks only too well.

15   For further details of *Liber Logaeth*, see section I of the present text.

16   All are in Dee's hand, with the exception of *Liber Mysteriorum Sextus et Sanctus* (*Liber Logaeth*), transcribed by Edward Kelly. They are contained in the following manuscript collections of the British Library: Sloane: 3188, 3189, Cotton Appendix MS. XLVI parts 1 & 2, and Sloane MS. 3191 respectively.

17   Sloane MS. 3677, 3678, etc.

18   *A True and Faithful Relation . . .* Meric Casaubon, London, 1659.

19   The original MS. is entitled *48 Claves Angelicae* (Sloane: 3191) indicating the term *Keys* to be correct.

20   Also referred to as *Mensa Faederis* (League Table or Table of Covenant). See Appendix B for illustration.

21   This short extract from the Call of the Thirty Aethers or Aires is taken from John Dee's *Eleventh Book of the Mysteries* (when taken in strict sequence) but is entitled: *Libri Septimi Apertorij Cracoviensis Mystici Sabbatici, Pars Quarta* (it begins 23 May 1584 and ends 12 July following). The column I have headed '*Pronunciation*' does not specifically fulfil this function, but furnishes the reader with some guidance and illustrates the manner in which words are divided and vowels stressed.

22   *The General and Common Exordium and Conclusion appertaining to the 7 Heptarchical Princes Inviting*. See *The Heptarchia Mystica of John Dee*, ed. Robert Turner, p. 63, Aquarian Press, 1986.

23   *The Complete Enochian Dictionary*, Donald C. Laycock, Preface by Stephen Skinner, Askin Publishers, London, 1978.

24   *The Heptarchia Mystica of John Dee*, pp. 104–5.

25   *The Complete Enochian Dictionary*, p. 19.

26   Ibid. On page 43 Laycock indicates the possible derivation of the angelic word *micaolz* (mighty) from the Scots *mickle*, which in fact means 'large in size or bulk, etc.'. The Scots word for mighty being: *michty* (*Concise Scots Dictionary*, ed. Mairi Robinson, Aberdeen University Press, 1987).

Ibid. page 173, the name *Thahaaotahe*, Supreme Elemental King of Earth (Golden Dawn derivation), is ascribed to *Water*.

The name *Thahebyobeeatan* (Water) is omitted from the above section.

Ibid. page 233, Laycock lists twenty-eight Seniors (Elders of the Apocalypse), when there are in fact twenty-four. His additional names are those of the four Tablet Kings: *Bataivah, Iczhhcal, Edelprna & Raagiosl*.

27   See *The Golden Dawn*, Israel Regardie, Llewellyn Publications, Minnesota, 1978, Vol. IV, p. 297.

28   A copy of this document can be found in the collection of the late Gerald Yorke (cf. Book 4, *The Golden Dawn*, I. Regardie). The complete manuscript, with comments, was published in *The Monolith*, Vol. 2, No. 5 (The Order of the Cubic Stone, Wolverhampton, England), 1983.

29   In his *Equinox* magazine Vol. 1, No. 7, Crowley renders the first, second and fourth names: TAHAOELOJ, THAHEBYOBEEÁTAN, OHOOOHAATAN respectively, and gives no instructions for their use (apart from a caution against the light use of these names). The Golden Dawn also remains silent in this matter.

30   A representation of this Seal can be found in Appendix B of the present volume. For further details regarding Sigillum Dei Aemeth see pp. 78–80 of my *Heptarchia Mystica of John Dee*.

JOHN DEE   *Courtesy of the Ashmolean Museum, Oxford*

I
John Dee
The Sage of Mortlake 1527–1608

"We are such stuff
as dreams are made on and our little life is rounded with a sleep."
(Prospero, in *The Tempest,* Act IV, Scene i)

In recent times much has been written in an effort to extol the virtues and talents of the celebrated Elizabethan Hermetic Scientist, Doctor John Dee. In this twentieth-century reassessment of Dee we can observe the slow, yet certain, re-emergence of a powerful and piercing intellect long neglected by academic posterity.

Much of Dee's former obscurity stems from his involvement in what is now known as occult practice and a misguided interpretation of the role of the Renaissance Magus. Heavily biased and ill-informed commentators, from the self-righteous Meric Casaubon[1] to the woolly-minded and credulous Thomas Smith[2] (and others), have done much to undermine the character of one of Tudor England's greatest worthies.

Amongst Dee's most recent biographers the work of the late Dr Peter French remains without parallel. In his *John Dee – The World of an Elizabethan Magus*[3] Dr French sets forth a scholarly account of the life and achievements of Dee against the background of Renaissance Angel magic and the Kabbalah. This method of portrayal succeeds admirably, and does much to disperse the air of charlatanism that has long sullied Dee's reputation.

In her learned series of books devoted to the philosophy of the *New Era*, the late Dame Frances Yates also flies to Dee's defence. Defining him as 'the leader of the Elizabethan Renaissance', she states: 'the old prejudices against him as a ludicrous figure still subsist, though very much diminished in force as it becomes more and more apparent that Dee had contacts with nearly everyone of importance in the age.'[4]

Frances Yates' statement is well borne out by the innumerable references in Dee's Diaries to such associates as: Gerard Mercator, Humphrey Gilbert, Martin Frobisher, Walter Raleigh, John Davis, Sir John Hawkins and the Queen herself. When one adds to this impressive list the host of foreign dignitaries, philosophers and mathematicians known personally to Dee, one cannot fail to gain some understanding of his sphere of influence.

Although John Dee claimed descent from the Welsh King Roderick the Great, his life began in fairly humble circumstances. Born on 13 July 1527, Dee entered a world on the verge of religious upheaval. The split with Rome was imminent and great and far-reaching changes were shortly to occur. For some of these revolutionary changes Dee was destined to be the instrument.

His parents, Roland Dee, a gentleman server at the court of Henry VIII, and his wife Joanna (daughter of William Wild) lavished great affection on their son, and although of slender income decided that he should receive a formal education. To this end he was sent to Chelmsford Grammar School, from where he passed in 1542, at the age of 15, to St John's College, Cambridge. He became Bachelor of Arts in 1544 and a Fellow in 1545. Later, after its foundation by Henry VIII, he became a founder fellow of Trinity College. Dee's brilliant academic career had begun.

In his twentieth year (1547) Dee embarked on the first of his many journeys to the Continent. On his return to Cambridge he took his Master's degree; but deciding to further his education abroad he left the following year and travelled to Louvain (Belgium) where he remained in such famous company as Gemma Frisius, Abraham Ortelius, Finaeus, Mercator and Pedro Nuñez, until 1550. Dee's travels then took him to Paris where (at the age of 23) he lectured on Euclid's Theorems to huge audiences.

On his return to England (1551) he secured the rectory of Upton-on-Severn in exchange for the annual pension granted to him under the Royal patronage of Edward VI. Dee had earlier (and wisely) dedicated two books to the young King.

After the untimely death of Edward (1553) and the accession of Mary Tudor (Bloody Mary), Dee's fortunes took a turn for the worse. In June 1555, he was thrown into prison and charged with treason and 'lewd and vain practices of calculating [casting nativities] or conjuring'. This imprisonment lasted only a few months, being almost immediately cleared of the first charge, but held for a time under custody to Bishop Bonner 'for examination in religious matters'. Dee conducted his own case with great authority and eloquence afforded by his vast and detailed knowledge of ecclesiastical matters, and in due course the charge of heresy was also dropped. His fellow prisoner Barthlet Grene was not so fortunate: he was burnt at the stake on the same accusations.

Although Dee's attention had been directed towards the Kabbalah, alchemy, astrology and angelic magic for some time, much of his reputation as a magician stemmed from his knowledge of the mechanical arts. During his period at Cambridge he was made responsible for the production of several classical plays. To enhance the performances he introduced various 'special effects' of a nature largely unwitnessed. These 'marvels', which made objects appear, disappear, and men fly through the air, although accomplished by way of levers, pulleys, wheels and such like, were in some cases held to have been achieved by the help of spirits 'whereat was great wondering and many vain reports spread abroad of the means how that was effected'.

On the morning of 17 November 1588 Mary died, and the Roman Church lost its last true foothold in England, regaining tenure only briefly during the reign of James II (1685–8). For John Dee and others of like mind a new age had truly begun: an age in which he was able to spread his philosophical and scientific wings without the hindrance of Papal restriction, and free from fear of religious persecution, to indulge his interests in alchemy and Kabbalistic Angel-magic.

The young Elizabeth summoned Dee to court and requested that he cast a horoscope in order to decide the most auspicious date for her coronation, which he set for 15 January 1589. The long and successful life of Elizabeth I will be seen by some as a fitting testimonial to her Astrologer. Dee remained devoted to his Queen throughout her reign, refusing to leave the Royal Service, despite the high honours and monetary awards offered to him by foreign princes. And although Elizabeth did not grant him a regular living until 1595 (the Wardenship of Manchester College) as a token of her esteem, she several times bestowed upon him gifts of money.

Dee married three times.[5] His first wife was Katherine Constable, the widow of a London grocer, who lived with him from 1565 until her death during 1574. The identity of Dee's second wife is unknown. He married her in 1575, but to his great loss, she died in the spring of the following year. In 1578 Dee took his third wife Jane Fromond, lady in waiting to the wife of Lord Admiral Howard. She bore all of his ten children (some authorities record eight) and remained at his side until her death by plague in 1605 (three years before his own death).

Shortly before 1570 Dee settled in Mortlake in Richmond-upon-Thames, at the house left to him by his mother. It was here in the rambling assembly of rooms and outbuildings that he gathered together what has been termed 'Elizabethan England's greatest Library'. His collection comprised almost three thousand printed books and one thousand manuscripts in various languages. The house suited Dee's needs admirably, for in addition to his literary collection, it adequately accommodated his many scientific instruments and afforded space for laboratory experimentation. Frequented by the learned of the age, Dee's home became an important centre for scientific thought and the furtherance of ideas. Apart from his various stays on the Continent Dee was to live out the remainder of his life in Mortlake, and was buried there in 1608 at the church of St Mary the Virgin.[6]

Any attempt even to summarise the extent and impact of John Dee's tremendous contributions to the navigational arts, mathematics, geography, philosophy, astronomy, and scientific thought of his age is quite beyond the scope of the present volume. It is hoped that some who have read this far will be persuaded to investigate these matters in further depth, and to this end I wholeheartedly recommend the works of the late Peter J. French[7] and E. G. R. Taylor.[8]

Dee's knowledge was not, it seems, won easily as he recalls of his earlier years at Cambridge:

> In the years 1543, 1544, 1545, I was so vehemently bent to studie, that for those yeares I did inviolably keepe this order; only to sleepe four houres every night; to allow to meate and drink (and some refreshing after) two houres every day; and of the other eighteen houres all (except the tyme of going to and being at divine service) was spent in my studies and learning.[9]

Dee's contributions to scientific and antiquarian literature were extensive, but with the exception of his *Hieroglyphic Monad*,[10] few of his works remain in print. Yet, like his Queen, Dee has received some degree of immortality through the writings of William Shakespeare. *The Tempest*[11] (written after Dee's death) indelibly engraves the archetypal image of the Elizabethan magus in the form of Prospero. Who but Dee could have formed so adequate a basis for the Bard's portrayal of the benign Agrippan sage, served by the dainty spirit Ariel? Who but Dee would so fervently wish to control the mariners' hostile and reluctant elements?

> And promise you calm seas, auspicious gales,
> And sail so expeditious, that shall catch
> Your royal fleet far off. [*Aside to Ariel*] My Ariel, chick,
> That is thy charge. Then to the elements
> Be free, and fare thou well!

> Prospero's final speech, *The Tempest*, Act V, Scene i.

Likewise, in a speech given by Oberon in *A Midsummer Night's Dream* (Act II, Scene ii), Queen Elizabeth is ensouled as the 'Virgin Queen':

Flying between the cold moon and the earth,
Cupid all arm'd: a certain aim he took
At a fair vestal throned by the west,
And loos'd his love-shaft smartly from his bow,
As it should pierce a hundred thousand hearts:
But I might see young Cupid's fiery shaft
Quench'd in the chaste beams of the wat'ry moon,
And the imperial vot'ress passed on,
In maiden meditation fancy-free.[12]

Although Dee's experiments with Angelic Magic began in his Cambridge days, it was not until his settlement in Mortlake that any real developments were to take place. His methodology and general approach to the subject seems to have centred on the use of various crystals and mirrors and the employment of earnest (Christian) prayer, coupled with the techniques set forth in Cornelius Agrippa's *Three Books of Occult Philosophy*.[13] As Dee (apart from one unaccountable instance) apparently lacked clairvoyant ability, he employed a number of Seers or Mediums in an effort to make contact with divine beings; he himself acting as recorder of the visions received.

From the records that have come down to us, it is obvious that Dee was both dissatisfied and dismayed with these early attempts to communicate with the Angels. The content of the received dialogue, lack of true consistency and general inferiority of the supposed communications all pointed towards deception on the part of the Seer. This suspicion was finally realised when Barnabas Saul (a lay-preacher and occultist), one of Dee's earliest scryers, first saw visions in the crystal and later (after some involvement with the law, perhaps on charges of sorcery), claimed that he had seen nothing.

This episode did not, however, dampen Dee's enthusiasm in his quest for contact with the intelligences of higher spheres. And shortly, to his own satisfaction at least, his ideal was to be achieved.

On 10 March 1582, Dee records in his *Liber Mysteriorum Primus* (The First Book of the Mysteries):

One Mr Edward Talbot cam to my howse, and he being willing and desyrous to see or show some thing of spirituall practise, wold have had me to have done some thing there in. And I truely excused my self therin as not in the vulgarly accounted Magik, neyther studies, or exercised: But confessed my self long tyme to have been desirous to have help in my philosophi-

call studies through the company and information of the blessed
Angels of God. And there uppon, I brought forth to him, my
stone in the frame (which was given me of a frende) and I sayed
to him, that I was credibly informed, that to it (after a sort) were
answerable Aliqui Angeli boni [Some Good Angels].

This encounter was to immediately cement a long-lasting relation-
ship.[14] On the same day Talbot (shortly to become Kelly), established
contact with what Dee undoubtedly believed to be the Archangel
Uriel. Following this an interchange takes place where Dee is
informed (via Talbot), that the Archangels Michael and Raphael are
also 'answerable' to the stone. Further (highly satisfactory, to Dee)
discourse then took place regarding Dee's mystical book SOYGA,
which was held to have been concerned with the revelations of
various Angels before the 'Fall from Paradise'.

After five months in Dee's employ, Talbot – somewhat abruptly –
changed his name to 'Kelly'. The reason for this is unknown, but Dee
always referred to him as E(dward)K(elly) henceforth.[15]

Kelly was almost 27 when he entered Dee's service (for the fee of
£50 per annum). Although born in Worcester, he was by nationality
Irish and the son of an apothecary. Little is known regarding Kelly's
movements prior to his arrival at Mortlake, but it is clear that he had
already gained some reputation as a magician, and had involved
himself in the nefarious art of necromancy.[16]

The early Angelic operations of Dee and Kelly gradually gained
momentum. Almost daily they sought contact with an ever growing
number of spiritual entities, and each 'action' (Dee's term for his
dealings with spirits) was recorded in minutest detail. Shortly they
were to receive instructions (from the spirits) regarding the construction of certain items of magical equipment. These requisites comprised the Holy Table (or *Table of Practice*); the Sigillum Dei Aemeth
(or *Sign of Truth*), a complex wax pentacle nine inches in diameter;
and the Seven Ensigns of Creation: seven talismans to be used in
conjunction with the Holy Table. (At first Dee is told to construct the
'Ensigns' from purified-tin, but is later instructed to paint them
directly upon the Table in blue lines and red letters.) Finally, a
Lamine (or magical breastplate) of parchment or paper is described.
(See Appendix B for further details of these ritual items.)

A magical ring, 'of the finest gold', is also mentioned. It was to
have a square or oblong bezel engraved with the name PELE (Hebrew:
'He who works wonders') and a central symbol. Although Dee is
told of the ring (via Kelly) 'WITHOUT THIS THOU SHALT DO NOTHING',[17]
it remains uncertain whether it was ever manufactured.

A new crystal – said to have been obtained from an Angel – was to be set in a frame of gold upon the Sigillum Dei Aemeth (a red silken cloth lay between), which in turn reposed upon the Holy Table. Four smaller versions of Sigillum Aemeth were – protected by wooden cases – placed beneath the legs of the Table.

From the extant manuscripts it is difficult to discover the exact manner in which this apparatus was meant to have been employed. It has even been suggested that Dee and Kelly never made practical use of the equipment they had so carefully constructed, being unable to understand the principle of its operation. Yet it is my personal belief that the Holy Table and other items were in fact employed in some of the later Actions, and evidence exists that along with the *Books of the Mysteries*, the Table, shew-stone and Sigillum Aemeth were often taken with them to the Continent.

After the emergence of the Heptarchial system of Planetary magic, events took a turn in another, quite different, direction. On 26 March 1582 Kelly produced an alphabet of twenty-one characters relating to what he held to be the language of the Angels. Dee records the reception of the alphabet in his *Fifth Book of the Mysteries*:

(E)dward (K)elly – he sheweth a boke, as he did before (all gold) and it is truth; whose truth shall endure for ever.

E.K: The leaves of the boke, are all full of square places, and thos Square place have Characters in them, some more than other: and they are all written with cullor, like blud, not yet dry. 49 square spaces, every way, were on every leaf. Which made in all, 2401, Square places. He wiped his finger on the top of the Table, and there cam out above the Table Certayn Characters enclosed in no lines: but standing by themselves, and points between them. He pointed orderly to them with his finger, and loked toward the skryer at every pointing.

Me [a female spirit of the Moon]: Note what they are.

(*a row of twenty-one characters are given here. See p. 22 for their final forms*)

(D)ee: They are noted.

E.K: He toke from under the Table, a thing like a great globe, and set that in the chayre and uppon that Globe layd a boke. He pointeth to the Characters: and cownteth them with his finger, being 21, and begynning from the right hand, towards the left. He putteth the Crown of gold, from his hed: and Layeth it, on the Table. His here *appereth* yellow. He maketh cursy: and *from under the Table taketh a rod* of gold in his hand, being divided into three distinctions.

He putteth the ende of the rod on the first of the Characters, and sayeth Pa and there appeared in english, or latin letters, *Pa*: he sayd *Veh*: and there appeared Veh in writting.[18]

CHARACTER	VALUE	NAME	CHARACTER	VALUE	NAME	CHARACTER	VALUE	NAME
ℨ	A	Un	ᙏ	H	Na	Ʊ	Q	Ger
V	B	Pa	⅂	I,Y	Gon	Ɛ	R	Don
I3	C,K	Veh	C	L	Ur	�	S	Fam
X	D	Gal	Ɛ	M	Tal	∕	T	Gisg
⅂	E	Graph	Ȝ	N	Drux	ⱥ	U,V	Van
ℱ	F	Or	L	O	Med	Γ	X	Pal
b	G,J	Ged	Ω	P	Mals	P	Z	Ceph

THE ANGELIC ALPHABET

Thus each letter of the Angelic Alphabet was named and assigned to its Latin equivalent. The first series of Characters (which must have been written down by Kelly) were crudely drawn, but later (6 May 1583) they appeared in 'yellow cullor' on one of the pages of *Liber Mysteriorum*. By drawing over these ghostly outlines in ink, Kelly arrived at the final highly stylised form of the Alphabet.[19]

Dee notes (on his return from London):

> But it is to be noted, that, when E. K. could not aptly imitate the forme of the Characters, or letters, as they were shewed: that then they appered down on his paper with a light yellow cullor, which he drew the blak uppon, and so the yellow cullor disapearing there remayned only the shape of the letter in blak.

Between 29 March and 6 April 1583 Dee and Kelly were engaged in writing the first section of the Angelicly transmitted book *Liber Logaeth*. This work (also known as *The Book of Enoch, Liber Mysteriorum Sextus (et Sanctus)*[20] and *The Book of the Speech of God*) consisted of firstly a series of Invocations in the Enochian or Angelic language, and secondly a large number (49×49) of squares containing letters and, in some instances, numbers. The exact method in which the book was delivered is, to say the least, confusing. Kelly's visions (as they are recorded) seem to indicate that each leaf of the book was held before him by the spirits and he read from them in turn, letter by letter. But as the actions run on he (after gaining permission from the spirits) forms words such as: 'Amidan gah lesco van gedon amchih ax or mandol cramsa ne dah vadge lesgamph ar: mara panosch aschedh or samhampore asco pacadabaah . . .', which Dee would have to record without knowledge of the involved spelling. Perhaps as this earlier version of the Angelic language lacked an English translation, Dee simply wrote the words as he heard them and disregarded their exact structure.

The Angels commanded that the entire *Liber Logaeth* must be written within forty days, and it was in fact completed on 6 May 1583, thirty-nine days after the reception of the first of these primary Angelic Invocations. Although the copy of *Liber Logaeth* (in Kelly's hand) is written in ordinary Latin letters, the Angels further instructed that the book was to be rewritten in the characters of the Angelic Alphabet and bound in silver – I can find no evidence to suggest that this was ever done, and on 16 August 1584 Dee writes: 'God he knoweth, and the Heavens, that I did the best I could, to have had the book silvered.'[21]

It seems that in some unknown manner the *Liber Logaeth* was used to generate the *Forty-eight Angelic Keys* system arising in later Actions. Indeed at the beginning of the section of the Spiritual Diaries dealing with the reception of these forty-eight Keys or 'Calls', Dee makes mention of the mystical book in his address to the Angel Nalvage (12 April 1584, at Cracovia): '(Dee to Nalvage) You mean the mystical Letters, wherein the holy book is promised to be written: and if the book be so written and laid open before us, and then you will from Letter to Letter point, and we to record your instructions.'[22] A series of most abstruse manoeuvres follow where dictated numbers are applied to the Tables of Liber Logaeth, employing a method that has not come down to us. The explanation fostered by the late Israel Regardie (and others of similar persuasion), that the dictated numbers simply refer to the 'rank and column' of a given square will be seen to be meaningless in the face of Angelic instructions such as: 'R The 43th. from the upper left angle to the right, and so still in the Circumference, 34006' or 'A 24th. from the Center ascending to the left angle, 25000.'[23] The most likely explanation is that some form of grid-system is involved, coupling the squares in a manner which could accommodate the many extremely high positional numbers. Whatever the answer, it is not to be found in the pages of *Liber Mysteriorum* or any other extant Dee manuscript.

The Angelic operations that took place between 13 April and 13 July 1584 resulted in the generation of three interlinked (in some places, somewhat tenuously) magical systems. They were, namely: *48 Claves Angelicae* (Forty-eight Angelic Keys), *Liber Scientiae Auxilii et Victoriae Terrestris* (The Book of Knowledge, Help and Earthly

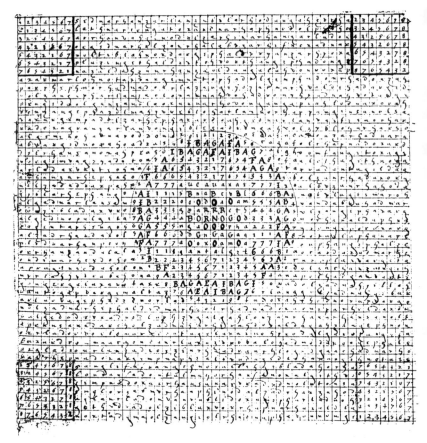

SQUARE FROM LIBER LOGAETH Sloane MS.3189 fol. 17r.

Victory), and *A Book of Supplications and Invocations*[24] (this book, in Latin, deals with the Invocation of the Angels who preside over the Four Quarters of the Terrestrial sphere).

These treatises, together with Dee's earlier *Heptarchia Mystica*, represent all that has survived of Dee's complete magical tracts. Their importance is reflected in the fact that fair copies of each book were made for easy reference, and that they were taken by Dee and Kelly on most of their travels.

The Book of the Forty-Eight Angelic Keys contains a series of 'Calls' or Invocations in the Angelic or Enochian language, together with an interlined English translation. These Calls were, in most cases, received letter by letter backwards in an attempt to prevent magical occurrences during their dictation. The English translations (mostly received at the same time) possess great poetic beauty, comparable in some instances to certain verses of the Apocalypse of Saint John. On this level the clairvoyant abilities of Edward Kelly have been extolled by many.

The Book of Knowledge, Help and Earthly Victory comprises a mass of tabulatory material connected with the Invocation and *modus operandi* of the system of the thirty Airs or 'Aethers'. It is directly associated with the final Call contained in *The Book of the Forty-Eight Angelic Keys* alongside which the names and division of the Aethers are given.

The Book of Supplications and Invocations is almost entirely based upon the manipulation of four alphabetic squares, their involved hierarchy of spirits, the ministry of the spirits, and the methodology of calling them forth. It is connected with *The Book of Knowledge, Help and Earthly Victory*, inasmuch as the sigils of the former are replicated in the squares.

Although the sophistication of these later communicated systems is apparent, it is strange to note that the only real practical example of Dee's employment of any of the transmitted techniques stems from his usage of earlier and unrefined *Heptarchia Mystica* (The Mysteries of the Sevenfold Kingdom).

The Heptarchial system is based upon a hierarchy of 'good Angels' all of which have names beginning with the letter B. Seven Kings, seven Princes and thirty-five lesser Angels are represented, rejoicing in such names (all of seven letters) as Baligon, Bornogo, Bapnido, Besgeme, etc. Dee collected the names of these forty-nine Angels together in a table which he called 'Tabula Angelorum Bonorum 49' (Table of 49 Good Angels). It was this Table that provided the basis for the only recorded example of talismanic magic to be drawn from the Angelic Actions. Furthermore, it seems that the characters of the Angelic Alphabet were employed here for the first time with any definite purpose.

Early in 1583 Dee petitions the Angel Murifri on behalf of two women, one afflicted in soul, the other in body. The first plea for help is upheld, the second refused on the grounds that it was requested in the interests of vanity.

The woman to receive help is Isabel Lister, of whom Dee states: 'the wicked Enemy has sore afflicted long with dangerous temptations, and hath brought her knives to destroy her self withall she resisteth hitherto.'

Murifri informs Dee that he will find his name under the numbers 49, 43, 35, 47, 9, 33, and 42[25] when applied to the positions indicated in his Table of Good Angels. This Dee accomplishes, but not without some difficulty as the number 35 did not yield the letter R in the first instance. (This first example was given purely to illustrate the way in which Dee was to utilise the Table.)

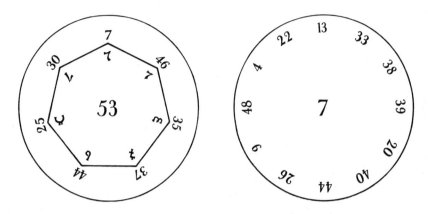

ISABEL LISTER'S TALISMAN

Later Dee is instructed to write down the numbers 7, 30, 25, 44, 37, 35, 46 representing (letter by letter) the word SOLGARS. Then adding the first and last numbers of the sequence, the number 53 is produced and in turn engraved within a septagon upon a plate of lead.

On the outer angles of the septagon the numbers corresponding to the word SOLGARS were to be engraved and on the inner angles the Angelic Characters of the same.

The obverse side of the Lamin, or talisman, was to bear the numerical equivalents of Isabel Lister's name[26] written in a circle about the number 7 (perhaps to indicate that the seventh table or column was used to generate the sequence of numbers).

All seems very complex and confusing until we employ Dee's Table of the 49 Good Angels and number the columns from left to right as shown on page 27.

The asterisks set against the letters in column three represent the numbers of the name SOLGARS,★ while those in column four furnish those of Isabel Lister's. Read horizontally each row of seven letters yields one of the Forty-nine Heptarchial names.

Dee is told (by Murifri) to apply the talisman to the afflicted woman's body as he thinks fit. No record of the talisman's effectiveness exists.

When Dee returned to England (after almost six years travelling in Europe) in 1589, Kelly remained in Prague to continue his alchemical experiments. They were never to meet again, although they occasionally corresponded and seem to have parted on friendly terms.

★ As the R in the name SOLGARS cannot be attributed to the number 35 in the third column, I have used the 33 twice in the above examples, being the nearest of seven possible alternatives. R.T.

	1	2	3	4	5	6	7
1	B	A	L	I	G	O	N
2	B	O	R	N	O	G	O
3	B	A	P	N	I	D	O
4	B	E	S	G	E	M	E★
5	B	L	U	M	A	P	O
6	B	M	A	M	G	A	L
7	B	A	S★	L	E	D	F
8	B	O	B	O	G	E	L
9	B	E	F	A	F	E	S★
10	B	A	S	M	E	L	O
11	B	E	R	N	O	L	E
12	B	R	A	N	G	L	O
13	B	R	I	S	F	L	I★
14	B	N	A	G	O	L	E
15	B	A	B	A	L	E	L
16	B	V	T	M	O	N	O
17	B	A	Z	P	A	M	A
18	B	L	I	N	T	O	M
19	B	R	A	G	I	O	P
20	B	E	R	M	A	L	E★
21	B	O	N	E	F	O	N
22	B	Y	N	E	P	O	R★
23	B	L	I	S	D	O	N
24	B	A	L	C	E	O	R
25	B	E	L★	M	A	R	A
26	B	E	N	P	A	G	I★
27	B	A	R	N	A	F	A
28	B	M	I	L	G	E	S
29	B	N	A	S	P	O	L
30	B	R	O★	R	G	E	S
31	B	A	S	P	A	L	O
32	B	I	N	O	D	A	B
33	B	A	R★★	I	G	E	S★
34	B	I	N	O	F	O	N
35	B	A	L	D	A	G	O
36	B	N	A	P	S	E	N
37	B	R	A★	L	G	E	S
38	B	O	R	M	I	L	A★
39	B	U	S	C	N	A	B★
40	B	M	I	N	P	O	L★
41	B	A	R	T	I	R	O
42	B	L	I	I	G	A	N
43	B	L	V	M	A	Z	A
44	B	A	G★	E	N	O	L★
45	B	A	B	L	I	B	O
46	B	U	S★	D	U	N	A
47	B	L	I	N	G	E	F
48	B	A	R	F	O	R	T★
49	B	A	M	N	O	D	E

Six years later (1595), Edward Kelly met his death while trying to escape from his imprisonment in the Bohemian castle of Zerner, where he had been held for some time after failing to provide the Emperor Rudolph with long-promised alchemical gold.

If Dee felt any grief at the final loss of his trusted seer, it is hardly discernible in his scant diary reference to Kelly's death: 'Nov. 25th, the newes that Sir Edward Kelly was slayne.'[27]

Although it seems likely that Dee continued to ponder the mysteries of his Angelic books, all serious attempts to communicate with the spirits were clearly abandoned after his parting with Kelly.

The death of Elizabeth (1603) heralded the most miserable period in Dee's long life. His beloved Queen gone, he now added to his ever-growing burden of ill health, poverty and old age (he was now 76) the ministrations of a new and unsympathetic monarch.

Dee's reputation as a magician still followed him. James I, author of the three-volume *Demonology* (shortly to become the witch-hunters' guide), looked upon Dee's religious Hermeticism with suspicion. To this king, all forms of magical art, natural, philosophical, or otherwise, were anathema and 'the assults of Satan'.

John Dee would never again receive the benefit of royal protection and favour he had so long enjoyed under Elizabeth. He died at his Mortlake home in 1608 comforted only by his devoted daughter Katherine and memories of a great age past.

> . . . Lend thy hand,
> And pluck my magic garment from me – So:
> Lie there my art.

> (Prospero, to Miranda, *The Tempest*, Act I, Scene ii)

Notes

1   Son of Isaac Casaubon. In 1659 he issued (with Preface) the later sections of John Dee's *Libri Mysteriorum* under the title: *A True and Faithful Relation of what passed for many Yeers Between Dr John Dee . . . and Some Spirits.*
2   See Thomas Smith, *Vita Joannis Dee in Vitae quorundam eruditissimorum et illustrium virorum*, London, 1707. Also *The Life of John Dee*, tr. from the Latin of Dr Thomas Smith, by Wm. Alex Ayton, London, 1908.
3   *John Dee – The World of an Elizabethan Magus*, Peter J. French, Routledge & Kegan Paul, London, 1972.
4   *The Occult Philosophy in the Elizabethan Age*, Frances A. Yates, London, 1979, p. 79.
5   See *Tudor Geography 1485–1583*, E. G. R. Taylor, Methuen & Co., London, 1930, p. 107 n. 1. Doctor Taylor indicates that information contained in Chancery Proceedings, Series II, Bundle 49, No. 44, relates to John Dee's first marriage.
6   See 'Mortlake Revisited', Robin E. Cousins, in *The Heptarchia Mystica of John Dee*, ed. R. Turner, pp. 107–15, Aquarian Press, 1986.

7 *John Dee – The World of an Elizabethan Magus*, Routledge & Kegan Paul, London, 1972.

8 *Tudor Geography*, E. G. R. Taylor, Methuen & Co., London (Reprinted, Octagon Books, Inc., New York, 1968).

9 Dee's *Compendious Rehearsal*, ed. T. Hearne (2 vols.), Oxford, 1726, pp. 5–6.

10 *The Hieroglyphic Monad*, tr. J. W. Hamilton Jones, London, 1947. See also *Monas Hieroglyphica*, tr. C. H. Josten, AMBIX, XII, 1964, London.

11 The earliest printed copy of *The Tempest* known is that in the folio published by Shakespeare's fellow-actors Heminge and Condell, in 1623, seven years after the poet's death. The first performance of this play is believed to have taken place on 'Hallowmas Night' (1 November), 1611.

12 With reference to this quotation, Mary Cowden Clarke makes the following comment: 'This is precisely one of those poetical compliments best calculated to please the royal Elizabeth, who loved to be called "the Virgin Queen", and to have her refusal of husband-suitors attributed to her being above the reach of passion-assaults. It is not to be supposed but that Her Majesty's woman-heart was accurately read by Shakespeare as those of all her sisterhood; and more delicate, as well as fancifully beautiful, verse-homage was never paid by writer to lady.' Mary Cowden Clarke, *The Plays of Shakespeare* (3 vols.), Vol. 1 (Comedies), Cassell, Petter & Galpin, London, Paris and New York, nineteenth century (illustrated by H. C. Setons).

13 *Three Books of Occult Philosophy*, Henry Cornelius Agrippa, tr. John French, 1651. Reprinted: Chthonios Books, London, 1986. Dee owned several copies of this book in the original Latin: *De Occulta Philosophia*, Henry Cornelius Agrippa Von Nettesheim, Antwerp, 1531.

14 For those interested in the art of Horary Astrology, Dee's first dealings with Talbot/Kelly as a scryer took place at 11.15 a.m., 10 March 1582, at Mortlake.

15 For further discussion on the theory of the 'alias' see my *Heptarchia Mystica*, pp. 20–1.

16 What scant information I have been able to assemble regarding Kelly's life and activities forms the substance of Appendix A.

17 *Heptarchia Mystica*, pp. 39, 75–6.

18 *Liber Mysteriorum Quintus*, 10 a.m., Tuesday, 26 March 1582 (Sloane MS. 3188 BL.).

19 See Sloane MS. 3188 BL. Folio 104 (*Quinti Libri Mysteriorum Appendix*).

20 Sloane MS. 3189 (BL) contains Edward Kelly's fair copy of this book.

21 *A True and Faithful Relation*, ed. M. Casaubon, p. 217.

22 Ibid., p. 78.

23 Ibid., p. 79.

24 As the fair copy (Sloane MS. 3191) of this book lacks a title page, I employ the name given by Elias Ashmole. R.T.

25 It seems that the third column of the Table is intended in this instance.

26   I S A B E L   L I S T E R
      13 33 38 39 20 40   44 26 9 48 4 22

27 *The Private Diary of Dr John Dee*, ed. James Halliwell, London, 1842, p. 54.

II
The Angelic Manuscripts

In 1662, fifty-four years after John Dee's death, his lost Angelic texts were discovered. They were found in a secret compartment of an old wooden chest by a London confectioner named Jones.[1] Although the finder did not understand the nature or significance of these manuscripts, and seemed uninterested in their content, he nonetheless retained them at his dwelling in Lumbard Street. Two years later Jones died (perhaps of plague) and, shortly after, his house was destroyed in the Great Fire of 1666. Fortunately, although the chest perished in the flames, the papers survived and were taken to Moon Fields by Mrs Jones[2] along with the rest of her goods. Later Mrs Jones married Thomas Wale (a Warden at the Tower of London), a close friend of Elias Ashmole. Wale soon realised that the papers were of some importance and, with his wife's permission, conveyed them to Ashmole for his opinion (Ashmole's deep interest in mystical and antiquarian matters was well known). The Wales subsequently offered to exchange the papers with Ashmole for his book on The Institution of the Garter, to which he readily agreed.[3]

Fate had indeed played a strange hand in restoring Dee's Angelic manuscripts to the world, yet one unfortunate incident mars the tale. While the papers were in the possession of Jones the confectioner, his housemaid saw fit to use half of the manuscripts in lighting fires, wrapping pies and other such uses. Of the content of these missing papers we can but speculate and conclude that certain elements of John Dee's Angel-magic may have been irretrievably lost.

The surviving manuscripts were received by Ashmole on 20 August 1672. They comprised (according to Ashmole): *Libri Mysteriorum I–V* (The first five books of the Mysteries); *The 48 Claves Angelicae*; *Liber Scientiae, Auxilii, et Victoriae Terrestris* (*The Book of Knowledge, Help and Earthly Victory*, A treatise on the 30 Aires); *A Book of Supplications and Invocations* (in Latin); and *De Heptarchia Mystica*.

Libri Mysteriorum I–V contain Dee's notes and observations on the early spiritual Actions which I have discussed in some detail above. They begin on 22 December 1581 and end in May 1583. *48 Claves Angelicae*, *Liber Scientiae* and the *Book of Supplications and Invocations* form the substance of the following section of this book. *De Heptarchia Mystica* I have published elsewhere (see Notes and Bibliography).

48 ANGELIC KEYS
Aᵒ 1584

Received (at divers times) from April 13th. to July 13th.
at Cracow
out of the mercy of our God to Whom alone we offer
all Praise, Honour and Glory,
Amen.[4]

Book 18

I

I	*rayng*	*over you*	*sayeth*	*the God*	*of Justice*
Ol	sonf	vorsg,	gohó	Iad	balt

in powre exalted	*above the firmaments*	*of Wrath:*
lansh	calz	vonpho,

in whose	*hands*	*the sonne*	*is*	*as*	*a sword,*
sobra	z-ol	ror	i	ta	Nazpsad

and the Mone	*as*	*a throwgh thrusting fire:*	*which*
Graa	ta	Malprg	Ds

measureth	*your garments*	*in the mydst*	*of my vestures*
hol-q	Qäa	nothóa	zimz

and	*trussed you together*	*as*	*the palms*	*of my hands:*
Od	commah	ta	nobloh	zien:

Whose	*seats*	*I garnished*	*with the fire*	*of gathering,*
Soba	thil	gnonp	prge	aldi

and	*beautified*	*your garments*	*with admiration*	*To whome*
Od	vrbs	óbŏleh	grsam	Casárm

I made a law	*to govern*	*the holy ones*	*and*	*delivered you*
ohoréla	cabá	pir	Od	zonrensg

a rod	*with*	*the ark of knowledge*	*moreover*
cab	erm	Iadnah	Pilah

you lifted up your voyces   *and sware*   Obedience   *and*
    farzm   zurza   adná   Ds

faith   *to him*   *that*   *liveth*   *and*   *triumpheth*   *whose*
gono   Iädpil   Ds   hom   Od   tóh   Soba

begynning is not,   *nor ende*   *can not be*   *which*   *shyneth*
  Ipam   lu   Ipămis   Ds   lóhŏlo

as a flame   *in the myddst*   *of your palace*   *and*   *reyngneth*
  vep   zomd   Poamal   Od   bogpa

amongst you   *as*   *the ballance*   *of righteousnes,*   *and*
  aäi   ta   piap   piamo-i   od

truth: *Move*   *therefore,*   *and*   *shew your selves*   *open*
vaoan   ZACARe   c-a   od   ZAMRAM   Odo

the Mysteries   *of your Creation.*   *Be frendly unto me:*
  ciclé   Qää   Zorge,

for   *I am*   *the servant*   *of the same your God*
Lap   zirdo   Noco   MAD

the true worshipper   *of the Highest.*
  Hoath   Iaida.

II

Can   *the wings*   *of the windes*   *understand*
Adgt   v-pă-ah   zongom   fa-á-ip

your voyces of wonder   *o you the second*   *of the first*
  Sald   vi-i-v   L

whome   *the burning flames*   *have framed*
sobam   I-ál-prg   I-za-zaz

within the depths of my Jaws   *whome*   *I have prepared*   *as*
  pi — ádph   cas-árma   abramg   ta

cupps   *for a wedding*   *or as*   *the flowres*   *in their beauty*
talho   parácleda   Q — ta   lors-l-q   turbs

for the Chamber   *of righteousnes*   *stranger*   *are*   *your fete*
  oŏge   Baltch   Giui   chís   lusd

then the barren stone:	*And*	*mightier*	*are*	*your voices*
orri	Od	mi-calp	chís	bia

then the manifold windes.	*For,*	*you are become*	*a buylding*
ózoňgon	Lap	noán	trof

such	*as is not*	*but*	*in the mynde*	*of the all powrefull*
cors	tage	o-q	manin	Ia-i-don

Arrise	*sayeth the First:*	*Move*	*therefore*	*unto his Servants:*
Torzú	góhel	ZACAR	ca	c-nó-qod,

Shew your selves	*in powre:*	*And*	*make me*	*a strong See-thing:*
ZAMRAN	micalzo	Od	ozazm	vrelp

for	*I am*	*of him that liveth for ever.*
Lap	zir	Ioiad.

III

Behold	*sayeth*	*your God,*	*I am*	*a Circle*	*on whose hands*
Micma	goho	Piad	zir	com-selh	a zien

stand	*12*	*Kingdoms.*	*Six*	*are*	*the seats*	*of living breath:*
blab	Os	Lon-doh	Norz	Chis	othil	Gigipah

the rest	*are*	*as sharp sickles:*	*or the horns*	*of death*
vnd-l	chis	ta-pu-im	Q mos-pleh	teloch

wherein	*the Creatures of ye earth*	*are*	*to*	*are*	*not*
Qui-i-n	toltorg	chis	i	chis	ge

Except	*myne own hand*	*which*	*sleep*	*and*	*shall ryse*
m	ozien	dst	brgda	od	torzul

In the first	*I made you*	*stuards*	*and*	*placed you*
i li	F ol	balzarg,	od	aala

in seats	*12*	*of government*	*giving*	*unto every one of you*
Thiln	Os	ne ta ab	dluga	vomsarg

powre	*succesively*	*over*	*.456*	*the true ages*	*of tyme*
lonsa	cap-mi-ali	vors	cla	homil	cocasb

to the intent that	*from ye highest vessells*	*and*	*the corners*
fafen	izizop	od	mi i noag

of	*your governments,*	*you might work*	*my powre:*
de	gnetaab	vaun	na-na-e-el

pouring downe	the fires of life, and encrease,	continually
panpir	Malpirgi	caosg

on the earth	Thus you are become	the skirts	of Justice
Pild	noan	vnalah	balt

and	truth	In the Name	of the same your God	Lift up
od	vooan	do o-i-ap	MAD	Goholor

I say	your selves.	Behold	his mercies	florish	and
gohus	amiran	Micma	Iehusoz	ca-ca-com	od

(his) Name	is become	mighty	amongst us.	In whome
do-o-a-in	noar	mi-ca-olz	a-ai-om	Casarmg

we say	I Move,	Descend	and	apply your selves unto us
gohia	ZACAR	vniglag	od	Im-ua-mar

as unto	the partakers	of the secret Wisdome
pugo	plapli	ananael

of your Creation.
Q a an.

IV

I have set	my fete	in the south	and	have looked abowt me;
Othil	lasdi	babage	od	dorpha

saying,	are not	the Thunders of encrease	numbered	33,
Gohol	G chis ge	auauago	cormp	pd

which raigne	in the second Angle?	under whome	I have placed
dsonf	vi v-di-v	Casarmi	oali

:9639:	whome	None	hath yet numbered	but one	in whome
Map m	Sobam	ag	cormpo	c-rp-l	Casarmg

the second beginning of things	are	and	wax strong
cro od zi	chis	od	vgeg

which also	successively	are	the number of time:
dst	ca pi mali	chis	ca pi ma on

their powers	are	as the first	:456:	Arrise
Ionshin	chis	ta lo	Cla	Torgu

you Sonns of pleasure,	and	viset the earth:	for
Nor quasahi	od	F caosga	Bagle

I am the Lord your God   which is,   and   liveth   In the name
    zi re nai ad   Dsi   od   Apila   Do o a ip

   of the Creator   Move,   and   shew your selves
    Q-a-al   ZACAR   od   ZAMRAN

  as pleasant deliverers   That you may praise him   amongst
    Obelisong   rest-el   aaf

      the sonnes of men.
      Nor-mo-lap.

V

  The mighty sownds   have entred   in ye third Angle   and
    Sa pah   zimii   du-i-v   od

are become   as olives   in ye olive mownt   looking with gladness
  noas   ta-qu-a-nis   adroch   dorphal

uppon the earth   and   dwelling   in the brightness of the hevens
  Ca ósg   od   faonts   peripsol

as contynuall cumforters   unto whome   I fastened
   tablior   Casarm   amipzi

pillars of gladness   :19:   and   gave them   vessels   to water
  na zarth   af   od   dlugar   zizop   z-lida

the earth   with her creatures   and   they are   the brothers
caosgi   tol torg   od   z-chis   e si asch

of the first   and second   and   the beginning
  L   ta vi u   od   iaod

of their own seats   which   are garnished   with continually
  thild   ds   peral

burning lamps   :69636:   whose   numbers   are   as   the first
  hubar   Pe o al   soba   cormfa   chis   ta   la

the endes   and   ye contents of tyme   Therefore   come you
  vis   od   Q-co-casb   Ca   nils

and   obey   your creation   viset us in peace   and
  od   Darbs   Q a as   Feth-ar-zi   od

  cumfort   Conclude us   as receivers   of your mysteries:
  bliora   ia-ial   ed nas   cicles

for why?   *Our Lord and Master*   *is all One.*
Bagle   Ge iad   i L

VI

The spirits   *of ye 4th. Angle*   *are*   *Nine,*   *Mighty*
Gah   s di u   chis   em   micalzo

in the firmament of waters: *Whome*   *the first*   *hath planted*
pil zin   sobam   El   harg

a torment   *to the wicked*   *and*   *a garland*   *to the righteous*
mir   babalon   od   obloc   samvelg

giving unto them   *fyrie darts*   *to vanne the earth*   *and*
dlugar   malprg   arcaosgi   od

7699:   *continuall workmen*   *whose course*   *viset with cumfort*
Acam   canal   so bol zar   f-bliard

the earth   *and*   *are*   *in government*   *and*   *contynuance*
caosgi   od   chis   a ne tab   od   miam

as the second   *and*   *the third*   *Wherefore*   *harken unto*
ta vi v   od   d   Darsar   sol peth

my voyce   *I have talked to you*   *and*   *I move you*
bi en   B ri ta   od   zacam

in powre and presence   *whose works*   *shalbe*   *a song of honor*
g mi calzo   sob ha hath   trian   Lu ia he

and the praise   *of your God*   *in your Creation.*
odecrin   MAD   Q a a on.

VII

The East   *is a howse*   *of virgins*   *singing praises*   *amongst*
R a as   isalman   para di zod   oe cri ni   aao

the flames of the first glory,   *wherein the· Lord*
ial purgah   qui in enay

hath opened his mowth: *and*   *they are become*   *: 28 :*
butmon   od   in oas   ni

Living dwellings   *in whome*   *the strength of man*   *rejoyseth*
  para dial   casarmg   vgear   chirlan

       and   *they are apparailed*   *with ornaments of brightness*
        od   zonac   Lu cif tian

   such as   *work wunders*   *on all creatures*   *Whose*   *Kingdoms*
   cors to   vaul zirn   tol ha mi   Soba   Londoh

and continuance   *are as the Third*   *and fourth*   *strong towres*
   od miam   chis tad   o des   vmadea

      and   *places of cumfort*   *The seats of Mercy*   *and continuance*
       od   pibliar   Othil rit   od miam

o you Servants   *of Mercy,*   *Move,*   *Appeare,*   *sing prayses*
  C no quol   Rit   ZACAR,   ZAMRAN   oecrimi

 unto the Creator: *And*   *be mighty*   *amongst us*   *For*
    Q a dah   od   o mi ca olz   aaiom   Bagle

to this rememberance   *is given*   *powre*   *and*   *our strength*
    pap nor   id lugam   lonshi   od   vmplif

       waxeth strong   *in our Cumforter.*
          vgegi   Bigliad.

VIII

The midday the first,   *is as*   *the third heaven*   *made*
    Bazmelo   i ta   pi ripson   oln

of Hyacinth Pillers   *:26:*   *in whome*   *The Elders*   *are*
   Na za vabh   ox   casarmg   vran   Chis

  become strong   *which I have prepared*   *for my own righteousnes*
     vgeg   dsa bramig   bal to ha

sayth the Lord   *whose long contynuance*   *shall be*   *as bucklers*
  goho i ad   solamian   trian   ta lol cis

to the stooping Dragon   *and*   *like unto the harvest*
   A ba i uo nin   od   a zi agi er

  of a wyddow.   *How many are there*   *which remayn*
     rior   Ir gil chis da   ds pa a ox

 in the glorie   *of the earth*   *which are*   *and shall not see*
    bufd   Caosgo   ds chis   odi puran

death   *until*   *this howse fall*   *and*   *the Dragon sink*
teloah   cacrg   isalman loncho   od   Vouina carbaf

come away,   *for*   *the Thunders,*   *have spoken:*   *Come away,*
Niiso   Bagle   auauago   gohon   Nilso

for   *the Crownes* *of the Temple,*   *and*   *the coat*
bagle   momao   siaion   od   mabza

of him that is,was, and shall be crowned,   *are divided*
Iad o i as mo mar   poilp

Come   *Appeare*   *to the terror*   *of the earth*   *and*
Niis   ZAMRAN   ci a o fi   caosgo   od

to our cumfort   *and*   *of such*   *as*   *are prepared.*
bliors   od   corsi   ta   a bra mig.

IX

A mighty   *gard*   *of fire*   *with two edged swords*   *flaming*
Mi ca oli   bransg   prgel   napta   ialpor

(which have viols :8   *of wrath*   *for two tymes*   *and*
ds brin efafafe P   vonpho   o l a ni   od

a half.   *Whose*   *wings,*   *are*   *of wormwood,*   *and*
obza   Sobca   v pa ah   chis   tatan   od

of the marrow   *of salt),*   *have setled*   *their feete*
tra nan   balye   a lar   lusda

in the west,   *and*   *are measured*   *with their Ministers*
so boln   od   chis hol q   C no quo di

:9996   *These*   *gather up*   *the moss*   *of the earth*   *as*
cial   v nal   aldon   mom   caosgo   ta

the rich man   *doth*   *his treasure:*   *Cursed*   *are they*
las ollor   gnay   limlal   Amma   chiis

Whose   *iniquities*   *they are*   *in their eyes*   *are milstones*
Sobca   madrid   z chis,   ooanoan   chiis auiny

greater than the earth   *And*   *from their mowthes*   *rane*
dril pi caosgin   od   butmoni   parm

seas of blud: *Their heds*   *are covered*   *with Diamond:*
zum vi C nila   Daziz   e thamz   a -childao

and uppon   *their heds*   *are*   *marble sleves.*   *Happy is he,*
od mirc   ozol   chis   pi di a i Collal   Vl ci nin

on whome   *they fown not.*   *For why?*   *The God of rytheousnes,*
a sobam   v cim   Bagle   Iad baltoh

rejoyseth   *in them.*   *Come away*   *and*   *not*   *your viols*
chirlan   par   Niiso   od   ip   ofafafe

For   *the tyme*   *is such as*   *requireth*   *cumfort.*
Bagle   acocasb   icorsca   unig   blior.

X

The Thunders of Judgment and wrath   *are*   *numbered*   *and*
Coraxo   chis   cormp   od

are harboured   *in the North*   *in the likeness*   *of an oak*
blans   Lucal   aziazor   paeb

whose   *branches*   *are*   *Nests*   *:22:*   *of lamentation*   *and*
soba   lilonon   chis   virq   op   eophan   od

weeping   *layd up*   *for*   *the earth*   *which*   *burn night*
raclir   maasi   bagle   caosgi   ds   ialpon dosiz

and day: *and vomit out*   *the heds*   *of scorpions*   *and*
od basgim   od oxex   dazis   siatris   od

live sulphur   *myngled*   *with poison*   *These be*
salbrox   cynixir   faboan   U nal chis

The Thunders   *that*   *:5678:*   *tymes*   *in ye 24th. part*
Coust   ds   saox   co casg   ol

of a moment   *roar*   *with a hundred mighty earthquakes*   *and*
oanio   yor   eors vohim gizyax   od

a thousand tymes   *as many surges*   *which*   *rest not*   *neither*
math cocasg   plo si molui   ds   pa ge ip   larag

know any   *echoing tyme.*   *Here*   *one rock*   *bringeth fortth*
om droln   matorb cocasb   emna   L patralx   yolci

1000   *even as*   *the heart*   *of man doth*   *his thoughts*
math   nomig   momons   olora gnay   angelard

Woe, Woe, Woe, Woe, Woe, Woe, yea,   woe   be to the earth
Ohio ohio ohio ohio ohio ohio noib   ohio   caosgon,

For	her iniquities	is		was	and shall be	great
Bagle	madrid	i		zirop	chiso	drilpa

Come awaye		but		not your noyses.
Niiso		crip		ip nidali.

XI

The mighty seat	groaned	and	they were	:5:	thunders
Ox i ay al	holdo	od	zirom	O	Coraxo

which flew	into the east	and	the Eagle	spake	and
ds zddar	ra asy	od	vab zir	comliax	od

cryed with a loud voyce	Come awaye	and they gathered
ba hal	Niiso	

themselves together and became the house of death
salman teloch

of whome	it is measured	and	it is as	they are
Casar man	hol-q	od	ti ta	z-chis

whose	number	is	:31:	Come away	For I prepare
soba	cormf	i	ga	Niisa	Bagle abramg

for you	Move	therefore	and	shew your selves
noncp	ZACARe	ca	od	ZAMRAN

open	the mysteries	of your creation	Be frendly unto me
odo	cicle	qaa	Zorge

for	I am	the servant	of ye same your God
lap	zirdo	noco	Mad

the true wurshipper	of the Highest.
Hoath	Iaida.

XII

O you	that rayng	in the sowth	and	are	:28:
Nonci	dsonf	Babage	od	chis	ob

the lanterns	of sorrow	bind up	your girdles	and	visit us
hubaio	tibibp	allar	atraah	od	ef

Bring down   your trayn   :3663:   that   the Lord
drix   fafen   Mian   ar   E nay

may be magnified   whose name amongst you   is   wrath
ovof   soba do o a   in aai   i   VONPH

Move,   I say,   and   shew your selves   open ye mysteries
ZACAR   gohus   od   ZAMRAM   odo cicle

of your Creation   be frendely unto me   for   I am   the servant
Qaa   Zorge,   lap   zirdo   noco

of the same your God.   The true wurshipper   of the Highest.
MAD   Hoath   Iaida.

XIII

O you swords   of the sowth   which have   :42:   eyes
Napeai   Babagen   ds brin   vx   ooaona

to stir up   the wrath   of synn   making   men   drunken
lring   vonph   doalim   eolis   ollog orsba

which are empty.   Behold   the promise   of God   and
ds chis affa   Micma   isro   MAD   od

his power   which   is called   amongst you   A bitter sting
lonshitox   ds   ivmd   aai   GROSB

Move   and   shew your selves   open   the mysteries
ZACAR   od   ZAMRAN,   odo   cicle

of your creation,   Be frendely unto me,   for I am the servant
Qaa,   zorge,   lap zirdo noco

of ye same your God   The true wurshipper   of the Highest.
MAD   Hoath   Iaida.

XIV

O you sonns   of fury   the daughters   of the Just   which
Noromi   bagie   pasbs   oiad   ds

sit   uppon   :24:   seats   vexing   all creatures
trint   mirc   ol   thil   dods   tolham

of the earth	with age	which have	under you	:1636:
caosgo	Ho min	ds brin	oroch	Quar

Behold the voyce	of God	the promise	of him
Micma bial	oiad	a is ro	tox

which is called	amongst you	Furye, or Extreme Justice
dsi vm	aai	Baltim

Move	and	shew your selves	open	the mysteries
ZACAR	od	ZAMRAN	odo	cicle

of your Creation	Be frendely unto me	for I am
Qaa,	zorge,	lap zirdo

the servant	of the same your God	the true wurshipper
noco	MAD,	hoath

of the Highest.
Iaida.

XV

O thou	the governor	of the first flame	under whose
Ils	tabaan	li al prt	casarman

wynges	are	:6739:	which weave	the earth
Vpahi	chis	darg	dso ado	caosgi

with dryness	which	knoweth	the great name	Righteousness
orscor	ds	omax	nonasci	Baeouib

and	the seal	of Honour	Move	and	shew yourselves
od	emetgis	iaiadix	ZACAR	od	ZAMRAM,

open the mysteries	of your Creation	Be frendely unto me
odo cicle	Qaa	zorge,

for	I am	the servant	of the same your God
lap	zirdo	Noco	MAD,

the true wurshipper	of the Highest.
hoath	Iaida.

XVI

O thou	*second flame*	*the howse*	*of Justice*	*which*
Ils	viuialprt	salman	blat	ds

hast thy begynning	*in glory: and*	*shalt cumfort*	*the Just*
acro odzi	busd od	bliorax	balit

which walkest	*on the earth*	*with feete*	*:8763:*
dsin-si	caosg	lusdan	Emod

that understand and	*separate creatures.*	*great*	*art*
dsom od	tli-ob	drilpa	geh

thou	*in the God of*	*stretch-forth and conquere*	*Move*
uls	MAD	zilodarp	ZACAR

and	*shew your selves*	*Open*	*the mysteries*	*of your creation*
od	ZAMRAN	odo	cicle	Qaa

Be frendely unto me,	*for*	*I am*	*the servant*
zorge,	lap	zirdo	noco

of the same your God	*the true wurshipper*	*of the Highest.*
MAD	hoath	Iaida.

XVII

O thou	*Third flame*	*whose*	*wynges*	*are thorns*	*to stir up*
Ils	di alprt	soba	vpa ah	chis manba	zixlay

vexation:	*and hast*	*:7336:*	*lamps living*	*going before*
dodshi	od brint	*Taxs*	hubaro	tas tax

thee	*whose God*	*is wrath in angre*	*gird up*	*thy loynes*
ylsi,	so bai ad	I von po vnph	Aldon	dax il

and	*harken*	*Move*	*and*	*shew your selves*	*Open*
od	toatar	ZACAR	od	ZAMRAM	odo

the mysteries	*of your Creation*	*Be frendely unto me*	*for*
cicle	Qaa	zorge	lap

I am	*the servant*	*of the same your God*	*the true wurshipper*
zirdo	Noco	MAD	hoath

of the Highest.
Iaida.

XVIII

O thou	*mighty light*	*and burning flame*		*of cumfort*
Ils	Micaol-z olprit	ial prg		Bliors

which	*openest*	*the glory*	*of God*	*to the centre*
ds	odo	Busdir	oiad	o uo ars

of the earth	*In whome*	*the secrets of truth*	*6332*	*have*
caosgo	Ca sar mg	La iad	eran	brints

their abiding	*which*	*is called*	*in thy*	*Kingdome*	*JOYE*
cafafam	ds	iumd	a q lo	a do hi	MOZ

and	*not to be measured*	*Be thou*	*a wyndow of cumfort*
od	ma of fas	Bolp	comobliort

unto me	*Move*	*and*	*shew your selves*	*Open*	*the mysteries*
pambt	ZACAR	od	ZAMRAN	odo	cicle

of your creation	*Be frendely unto me*	*for I am*	*the servant*
Qaa	zorge	lap zirdo	Noco

of the same your God	*the true wurshipper*	*of the Highest.*
MAD	Hoath	Iaida.

XIX
The Key of the Thirty Aires

O you hevens	*which dwell*	*in the first Ayre,*	*are*	*Mightie*
Madriax	ds praf	LIL*	chis	Micaolz

in the parts	*of the Earth,*	*and execute*	*the Judgment*
saanir	caosgo	od fisis	bal zizras

of the highest:	*to you it is said,*	*Behold*	*the face*
Iaida	nonca gohulim	Micma	adoian

of your God,	*the begynning*	*of cumfort;*	*whose eyes*
MAD	I a od	bliorb	sa ba ooaona

are	*the brightness*	*of the hevens:*	*which*	*provided*	*you*
chis	Luciftias	peripsol	ds	abraassa	noncf

for the government	*of the Earth,*	*and*	*her*	*unspeakab*
netaa ib	caosgi	od	tilb	adphaht

*This name is to be varied with the nature of the Aire invoked.

variety *furnishing* *you* *with a power of understanding*
dam ploz tooat noncf gmi calzoma

to dispose *all things* *according* *to the providence*
L rasd tofglo marb yarry

of him that sitteth on the Holy Throne *and* *rose up*
I DOI GO od tor zulp

in the begynning, *saying,* *The Earth let her be governed*
ia o daf gohol caosga ta ba ord

by her parts *and* *let there be* *Division* *in her*
saanir od christeos yr poil ti ob l

that the glory of her *may be* *allwayes* *drunken* *and*
Bus dir tilb noaln pa id orsba od

vexed *in itself:* *Her course,* *let it run*
dodrmni zylna El zap tilb parm gi

with the hevens: *and* *as* *a handmayd* *Let her serve them:*
pe rip sax od ta qurlst bo o a pi S

One season *let it confownd another:* *And let there be*
L nib m ov cho symp od Christeos

no Creature *uppon,* *or within her,* *the same:* *All*
Ag tol torn mirc q ti ob l Lel, Tom

her members *let them differ* *in their qualities:* *And*
paombd dilzmo aspian, Od

let there be *no one Creature* *equal* *with another:*
christeos Ag L tor torn parach a symp,

The reasonable Creatures of the Earth *let them vex*
Cord ziz dod pal

and weede out *one another:* *And* *the dwelling places*
od fifalz L s mnad, od fargt

let them forget *their names:* *The work of man,* *and*
bams omaoas Conisbra od

his pomp, *let them be defaced:* *His buildings*
auauox tonug Ors cat bl

let them become *caves* *for the beasts of the field:*
noasmi tab ges Leuith mong

Confownd   *her understanding*   *with darkness.*   *For why?*
vnchi   omp tilb   ors.   Bagle

It repenteth me   *I made man.*   *One while*   *let her be known,*
Mo o o ah   ol cord ziz   L ca pi ma o   ix o maxip

and another while   *a stranger:*   *Because*   *she is*   *the bed*
od ca co casb   gosaa   Baglen   pi i   tianta

of a Harlot,   *and the*   *dwelling place*   *of him that is fallen:*
a ba ba lond   od   faorgt   teloc vo v im

O you heavens,   *arrise,*   *the lower heavens*   *under neath you,*
Ma dri iax   torzu   o adriax   oro cha

Let them serve you: *Govern*   *those that govern:*   *Cast down*
aboapri   Tabaori   priaz ar ta bas.   A dr pan

such as   *fall:*   *Bring forth*   *with those*   *that encrease:*
cor sta   dobix   Yol cam   pri a zi   ar coazior.

And destroy   *the rotten:*   *No place*   *let it remayne*
Od quasb   q ting   Ripir   pa a oxt

in one number.   *Add*   *and Diminish,*   *untill*   *the stars*
sa ga cor.   vm l   od prd zar   ca crg   A oi ve a e

be numbered: ARRISE,   MOVE,   *and*   APPEAR   *before*
cormpt   TORZV   ZACAR   od   ZAMRAN   aspt

the Covenant   *of his mowth,*   *which*   *he hath sworne unto us,*
sibsi   but mona   ds   surzas tia

in his Justice: OPEN   *the Mysteries*   *of your Creation:*
baltan   ODO   cicle   Qaa

And   *Make us*   *partakers*   *of undefyled Knowledge.*
Od   Ozazma   plapli   Iad na mad.

The Thirty Names of the Aires

1. Lil	6. Maz	11. Ich	16. Lea	21. Asp	26. Des
2. Arn	7. Deo	12. Loe	17. Tan	22. Lin	27. Zaa
3. Zom	8. Zid	13. Zim	18. Zen	23. Tor	28. Bag
4. Paz	9. Zip	14. ·Vta	19. Pop	24. Nia	29. Rii
5. Lat	10. Zax	15. Oxo	20. Chr	25. Vti	30. Tex

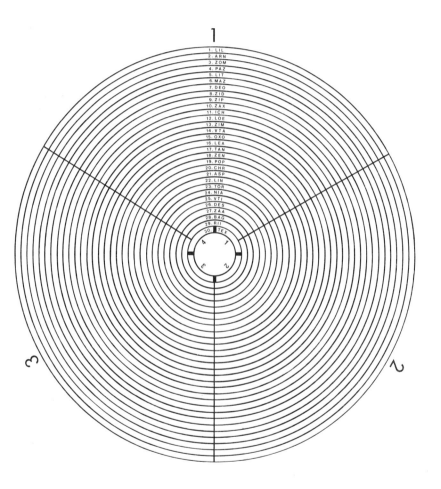

THE THIRTY AIRES

THE BOOK OF KNOWLEDGE
HELP AND EARTHLY VICTORY
A°1585
May 2°

(New style)
Cracow in Poland[5]

Note

In the original manuscript, each column of correspondences is headed with a lengthy title in Latin. For technical reasons we have been unable to adopt this system of notation in the present volume; and have therefore utilised a series of Roman numerals to represent each column in accordance with the following key:

I: A continuous series of 91 parts.
II: 91 Names of the parts of the earth imposed by men.
III: 91 Names of the parts of the earth divinely given.
IV: 91 symmetrical characters divinely given.
V: 30 Spheric orders of good princes of the air.
VI: Tripartite number of the good servants of each order.
VII: Total number of the tripartite good servants in each order.
VIII: 12 Angel Kings ruling their 30 orders, who are over 12 tribes also.
IX: 12 Tribes of the Israelite people at the dispersal.
X: 4 Zones of the world assigned to the dispersed tribes.[6]

Special Note on Column X

The zones of the world assigned to the Twelve Dispersed Tribes of Israel do not (as certain commentators have indicated) represent the usual points of the compass: North, South, East, West, North N-W, East N-E, etc. The key to Dee's intended directions can be clearly found in the second diagram he appends to his manuscript (given here on p. 58). The diagram is representative of the order of the Tribes at their dispersal (and indeed in 1585) drawn within the walls of the Holy City. To interpret Dee's intentions it is necessary to imagine oneself viewing a particular wall of the city from the *outside*. Then following the directive with reference to the relevant diagram the meaning becomes obvious. E.g. 'On the East side, to the right-hand = NAPHTALI (*Dee: Oriens-dexter=Nephthalim*); on the West side, to the left-hand = ISSACHAR (*Dee: Occidens-sinister=Isacaraah*); to the North = MANASSEH (*Dee: Aquilonaris=Manasse*) etc.' Therefore in each instance the direction in which one is facing (i.e. towards a particular wall of the city) would be geographically opposite the Cardinal point named in this column (X).

In the present transcription I have represented the points of the compass (North, South, East and West) in the conventional manner, i.e. by their initial letters: N, S, E, W (Dee MS: *Aquilonaris, Meridies, Oriens, Occidens – Lat.*), and the directions Left and Right by the letters L and R respectively. Thus E-L signifies 'Looking towards the Eastern wall (of the Holy City), to the Left-hand side', etc.

THE BOOK OF KNOWLEDGE, HELP AND EARTHLY VICTO

When the Most High divided to the nations their inheritance, whe
he separated the sons of Adam, he set the bounds of the peop
according to the number of the children of Israel.

The song of Moses, Deuteronomy, 32

I	II	III	IV	V	V
1	Aegyptus	Occodon	⟨sigil⟩	Order	7.
2	Syria	Pascomb	⟨sigil⟩	1	2.
3	Mesopotamia	Valgars	⟨sigil⟩	LIL	5.
4	Cappadocia	Doagnis	⟨sigil⟩	Order	3(
5	Tuscia	Pacasna	⟨sigil⟩	2	2.
6	Parva Asia	Dialiva	⟨sigil⟩	ARN	8(
7	Hyrcania	Samapha	⟨sigil⟩	Order	4.
8	Thracia	Virooli	⟨sigil⟩	3	3(
9	Gosmam	Andispi	⟨sigil⟩	ZOM	9.
10	Thebaidi	Thotanp	⟨sigil⟩	Order	2.
11	Parsadal	Axziarg	⟨sigil⟩	4	3(
12	India	Pothnir	⟨sigil⟩	PAZ	6.
13	Bactriane	Lazdixi	⟨sigil⟩	Order	8(
14	Cilicia	Nocamal	⟨sigil⟩	5	2.
15	Oxiana	Tiarpax	⟨sigil⟩	LIT	5(
16	Numidia	Saxtomp	⟨sigil⟩	Order	3(
17	Cyprus	Vauaamp	⟨sigil⟩	6	9.
18	Parthia	Zirzird	⟨sigil⟩	MAZ	7.

And had a wall great and high, and had twelve gates, and at the gates twelve ANGELS, and names written thereon, which are the names of the twelve tribes of the children of Israel:

Revelation: Chapter 21.[8]

VII	VIII		IX	X
	9★	ZARZILG	Naphtali	E–R
14931	11	ZINGGEN	Zebulun	W–R
	7	ALPVDUS	Issachar	W–L
	4	ZARNAAH	Manasseh	N
15960	2	ZIRACAH	Reuben	S
	2	ZIRACAH	Reuben	S
	9	ZARZILG	Naphtali	E–R
17296	7	ALPVDUS	Issachar	W–L
	10	LAVAVOTH	Gad	S–R
	10	LAVAVOTH	Gad	S–R
11660	10	LAVAVOTH	Gad	S–R
	12	ARFAOLG	Ephraim	N–R
	1	OLPAGED	Dan	E
16738	7	ALPVDUS	Issachar	W–L
	11	ZINGGEN	Zebulun	W–R
	5	GEBABAL	Asher	E–L
20040	12	ARFAOLG	Ephraim	N–R
	5	GEBABAL	Asher	E–L

★Denotes number of Tribe.

I	II	III	IV	V	VI
19	Getulia	Opmacas		Order	6363
20	Arabia	Genadol		7	7706
21	Phalagon	Aspiaon		DEO	6320
22	Mantiana	Zamfres		Order	4362
23	Soxia	Todnaon		8	7236
24	Gallia	Pristac		ZID	2302
25	Illyria	Oddiorg		Order	9996
26	Sogdiana	Cralpir		9	3620
27	Lydia	Doanzin		ZIP	4230
28	Caspis	LEXARPH		Order	8880
29	Germania	COMANAN		10	1230
30	Trenam	TABITOM		ZAX	1617
31	Bithynia	Molpand		Order	3472
32	Graecia	Vsnarda		11	7236
33	Licia	Ponodol		ICH	5234
34	Onigap	Tapamal		Order	2658
35	India Major	Gedoons		12	7772
36	Orcheny	Ambriol		LOE	3391
37	Achaia	Gecaond		Order	8111
38	Armenia	Laparin		13	3360
39	Cilicia	Docepax		ZIM	4213
40	Paphlagonia	Tedoond		Order	2673
41	Phasiana	Viuipos		14	9236
42	Chaldei	Ooanamb		VTA	8230

VII	VIII		IX	X
	4	ZARNAAH	Manasseh	N
20389	3	HONONOL	Judah	W
	11	ZINGGEN	Zebulun	W–R
	5	GEBABAL	Asher	E–L
13900	1	OLPAGED	Dan	E
	9	ZARZILG	Naphtali	E–R
	3	HONONOL	Judah	W
17846	10	LAVAUOTH	Gad	S–R
	9	ZARZILG	Naphtali	E–R
	11	ZINGGEN	Zebulun	W–R
11727	7	ALPVDUS	Issachar	W–L
	9	ZARZILG	Naphtali	E–R
	10	LAVAUOTH	Gad	S–R
15942	6	ZVRCHOL	Simeon	S–L
	3	HONONOL	Judah	W
	6	ZVRCHOL	Simeon	S–L
13821	8	CADAAMP	Benjamin	N–L
	2	ZIRACAH	Reuben	S
	10	LAVAVOTH	Gad	S–R
15684	1	OLPAGED	Dan	E
	7	ALPVDUS	Issachar	W–L
	5	GEBABAL	Asher	E–L
20139	7	ALPVDUS	Issachar	W–L
	12	ARFAOLG	Ephraim	N–R

I	II	III	IV	V	VI
43	Itergi	Tahando	◈	Order	136
44	Macedonia	Nociabi	◈	15	136
45	Garamantica	Tastoxo	◈	OXO	188
46	Sauromatica	Cucarpt	◈	Order	992
47	Aethiopia	Luacon	◈	16	923
48	Fiacim	Sochial	◈	LEA	924
49	Colchica	Sigmorf	◈	Order	762
50	Cireniaca	Aydropt	◈	17	173
51	Nasamonia	Tocarzi	◈	TAN	263
52	Carthago	Nabaomi	◈	Order	234
53	COXLANT	ZAFASAI	◈	18	768
54	Idumea	Yalpamb	◈	ZEN	927
55	Parstavia	Torzoxi	◈	Order	623
56	Celtica	Abaiond	◈	19	673
57	Vinsan	Omagrap	◈	POP	238
58	Tolpam	Zildron	◈	Order	362
59	Carcedonia	Parziba	◈	20	762
60	Italia	Totocan	◈	CHR	363
61	Brytania	Chirspa	◈	Order	553
62	Phenices	Toantom	◈	21	563
63	Comaginen	Vixpadg	◈	ASP	565
64	Apulia	Ozidaia	◈	Order	223
65	Marmarica	PARAOAN	◈	22	232
66	Concava-Syria	Calzidg	◈	LIN	236

VII	VIII		IX	X
	9	ZARZILG	Naphtali	E–R
4620	10	LAVAVOTH	Gad	S–R
	12	ARFAOLG	Ephraim	N–R
	2	ZIRACAH	Reuben	S
28390	3	HONONOL	Judah	W
	12	ARFAOLG	Ephraim	N–R
	2	ZIRACAH	Reuben	S
	1	OLPAGED	DAN	E
	9	ZARZILG	Naphtali	E–R
	5	GEBABAL	Asher	E–L
19311	7	ALPVDUS	Issachar	W–L
	12	ARFAOLG	Ephraim	N–R
	12	ARFAOLG	Ephraim	N–R
15356	8	CADAAMP	Benjamin	N–L
	11	ZINGGEN	Zebulun	W–R
	5	GEBABAL	Asher	E–L
14889	3	HONONOL	Judah	E
	7	ALPVDUS	Issachar	W–L
	12	ARFAOLG	Ephraim	N–R
16829	8	CADAAMP	Benjamin	N–L
	6	ZVRCHOL	Simeon	S–L
	12	ARFAOLG	Ephraim	N–R
6925	1	OLPAGED	Dan	E
	12	ARFAOLG	Ephraim	N–R

I	II	III	IV	V	V
67	Gebal	Ronoamb	⌐	Order	7
68	Elam	Onizimp	⊐	23	7
69	Idunia	Zaxanin	⌐	TOR	7
70	Media	Orcanir	⌐⌐	Order	8
71	Ariana	Chialps	⌐⌐	24	8
72	Chaldea	Soageel	⌐	NIA	8
73	Sericipopuli	Mirzind	⌐	Order	5
74	Persia	Obuaors	⌐	25	6
75	Gongatha	Ranglam	⌐	VTI	6
76	Gorsim	Pophand	⌐⌐	Order	9
77	Hispania	Nigrana	⌐	26	3
78	Pamphilia	Bazchim	⌐	DES	5
79	Oacidi	Saziami	⌐	Order	7
80	Babylon	Mathula	⌐	27	7
81	Median	Orpamb	⌐	ZAA	7
82	Idumian	Labnixp	⌐	Order	2
83	Felix Arabia	Focisni	⌐	28	7
84	Metagonitidim	Oxlopar	⌐	BAG	8
85	Assyria	Vastrim	⌐	Order	9
86	Affrica	Odraxti	⌐	29	4
87	Bactriani	Gomziam	⌐	RII	7
88	Afran	Taoagla	⌐	Order	4
89	Phrygia	Gemnimb	⌐	30	9
90	Creta	Advorpt	⌐⌐	TEX	7
91	Mauritania	Dazinal	⌐		5

VII	VIII		IX	X
	4	ZARNAAH	Manasseh	N
21915	10	LAVAVOTH	Gad	S–R
	11	ZINGGEN	Zebulun	W–R
	4	ZARNAAH	Manasseh	N
24796	10	LAVAVOTH	Gad	S–R
	11	ZINGGEN	Zebulun	W–R
	4	ZARNAAH	Manasseh	N
18201	2	ZIRACAH	Reuben	S
	12	ARFAOLG	Ephraim	N–R
	12	ARFAOLG	Ephraim	N–R
18489	8	CADAAMT	Benjamin	N–L
	12	ARFAOLG	Ephraim	N–R
	2	ZIRACAH	Reuben	S
22043	4	ZARNAAH	Manasseh	N
	5	GEBABAL	Asher	E–L
	10	LAVAVOTH	Gad	S–R
18066	9	ZARZILG	Naphtali	E–R
	6	ZVRCHOL	Simeon	S–L
	3	HONONOL	Judah	W
21503	4	ZARNAAH	Manasseh	N
	12	ARFAOLG	Ephraim	N–R
	12	ARFAOLG	Ephraim	N–R
27532	4	ZARNAAH	Manasseh	N
	3	HONONOL	Judah	W
	6	ZVRCHOL	Simeon	S–L

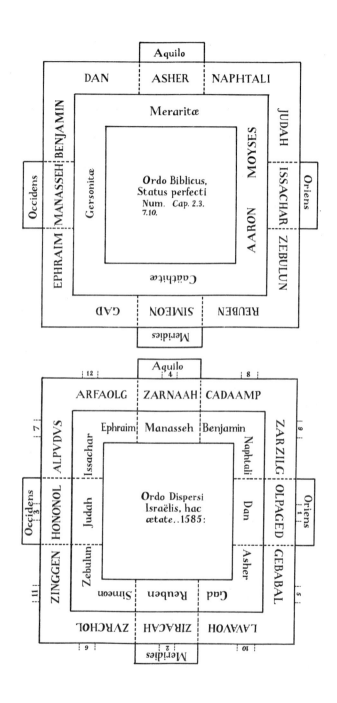

A BOOK OF SUPPLICATIONS AND INVOCATIONS[9]

```
r Z i l a f A y t I p a e b O a Z a R o p h a R a
a r d Z a i d p a L a m u N n a x o P S o n d n
c z o n s a r o Y a u b x a i g r a n o o m a g g
T o i T t z o P a c o C a o r p m n i n g b e a l
S i g a s o m r b z n b r r s O n i z i r l e m u
f m o n d a T d i a r i p i z i n r C z i a M h l
o r o i b A h a o z p i M O r d i a l h C t G a
t N a b r V i x g a s d h o c a n c h i a s o m t
O i i i t T p a l O a i A r b i z m i i l p i z
A b a m o o o a C u c a C O p a n a b a m S m a P
N a o c O T t n p r n T o d O l o P i n i a n b a
o c a n m a g o t r o i m r x p a o c s i z i x p
S h i a l r a p m z o x a a x t i r V a s t r i m
m o t i b   a T n a n   n a n T a   b i t o m
d o n p a T d a n V a a a T a O A d u p t D n i m
o l o a G e o o b a u a a a b c o o r o m e b b
O P a m n o V G m d n m m T o g c o n x m a l G m
a p l s T e d e c a o p o n h o d D i a l e a o c
s c m i o o n A m l o x C p a t A x i o V s P s M
V a r s G d L b r i a p h S a a i x a a r V r o i
o i p t e a a p D o c e m p h a r s l g a i o l
p s u a c N r Z i r Z a p M a m g l o i n L i r x
S i o d a o i n r z f m o l a a D n g a T a p a
d a l_b t T d n a d i r e r p a L c o i d x P a c n
d i x o m o n s i o s p a n d a z N z i V a a s a
O o D p z i A p a n l i x i i d P o n s d A s p i
r g o a n n q A C r a r e x r i n h t a r a d J
```

THE ANGELIC TABLE

r	Z	i	l	a	f	A	y	t	l	p	a	e	T	a	O	A	d	v	p	t	D	n	i	m
a	r	d	Z	a	i	d	p	a	L	a	m		a	a	b	c	o	o	r	o	m	e	b	b
c	z	o	n	s	a	r	o	Y	a	v	b	x	T	o	g	c	o	n	x	m	a	l	G	m
T	o	i	T	t	z	o	P	a	c	o	C	a	n	h	o	d	D	i	a	l	e	a	o	c
S	i	g	a	s	o	m	r	b	z	n	h	r	p	a	t	A	x	i	o	V	s	P	s	И
f	m	o	n	d	a	T	d	i	a	r	i	p	S	a	a	i	x/p	a	a	r	V	r	o	i
o	r	o	i	b	A	h	a	o	z	p	i		m	p	h	a	r	s	l	g	a	i	o	l
t	N	a	b	r	V	i	x	g	a	s	d	h	M	a	m	g	l	o	i	n	L	i	r	x
O	i	i	i	t	T	p	a	l	O	a	i		o	l	a	a	D	n	g	a	T	a	p	a
A	b	a	m	o	o	o	a	C	u	c	a	C	p	a	L	c	o	i	d	x	P	a	c	n
N	a	o	c	O	Tt	t/T	n	p	r	n	T	o	n	d	a	z	N	z	i	V	a	a	s	a
o	c	a	n	m	a	g	o	t	r	o	i	m	i	i	d	P	o	n	s	d	A	s	p	i
S	h	i	a	l	r	a	p	m	z	o	x	a	x	r	i	n	h	t	a	r	n	d	i	⅃
m	o	t	i	b			a	T	n	a	n		n	a	n	T	a			b	i	t	o	m
b	O	a	Z	a	R	o	p	h	a	R	a+	a	d	o	n	p	a	T	d	a	n	V	a	a
u	N	n	a	x	o	P	S	o	n	d	n		o	l	o	a	G	e	o	o	b	a	u	a
a	i	g	r	a	n	o	o	m	a	g	g	m	O	P	a	m	n	o	V	G	m	d	n	m
o	r	p	m	n	i	n	g	b	e	a	l	o	a	p	l	s	T	e	d	e	c	a	o	p
r	s	O	n	i	z	i	r	l	e	m	v	C	s	c	m	i	o	o	n	A	m	l	o	x
i	z	i	n	r	C	z	i	a	M	h	l	h	V	a	r	s	G	d	L	b	r	i	a	p
M	O	r	d	i	a	l	h	C	t	G	a		o	i	P	t	e	a	a	p	D	o	c	e
⊙	c	a	n	c	h	i	a	s	o	m	t	p	p	s	u	a	c	N	r	Z	i	r	Z	a
A	r	b	i	z	m	i	i	l	p	i	z		S	i	o	d	a	o	i	n	r	z	f	m
O	p	a	n	a	l	a	m	S	m	a	P	r	d	a	lb	t	T	d	n	a	d	i	r	e
d	O	l	o	P	i	n	i	a	n	b	a	a	d	i	x	o	m	o	n	s	i	o	s	p
r	x	p	a	o	c	s	i	z	i	x	p	x	O	o	D	p	z	i	A	p	a	n	l	i
a	x	t	i	r	V	a	s	t	r	i	m	e	r	g	o	a	n	n	q	A	C	r	a	r

THE ANGELIC TABLE (REFORMED)

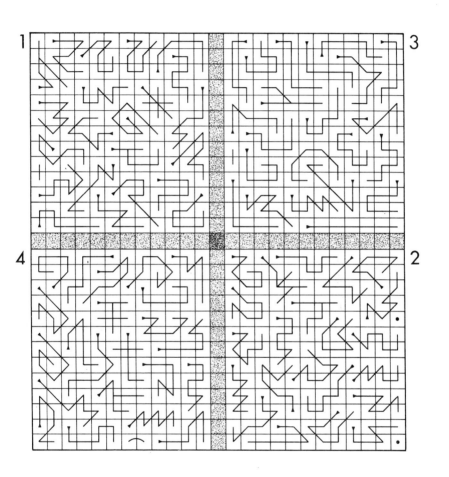

'THE 91 SYMMETRICAL CHARACTERS'

✝

Fundamentalis ad DEVM Supplicatio, et Obtestatio pro Angelorum Bonorum, benigno, habendo Ministerio

O Ieova Zebaoth, Diuinam tuam Potentiam, Sapientiam, et Bonitatem, enixissime supplico et imploro (Ego Ioannes Dee, Seruulus tuus indignus) et mihi semper fauorabilem, assistentem esse, humillime, et fideliter peto: in omnibus meis factis, Verbis et Cogitationibus, laudem, honorem et gloriam tuam concernentibus, promouentibus vel procurantibus: Et per hæc 12. Mystica Nomina tua, ORO, IBAH, AOZPI, MOR, DIAL, HCTGA, OIP, TEAA, PDOCE, MPH, ARSL, GAIOL, Diuinam et Omnipotentem Maiestatem tuam ardentissime Obtestor et Obsecro: Vt fideles omnes tui Spiritus Angelici (quorum Mystica Nomina, hoc libro continentur expressa, breuissimeq́ notantur Officia,) in quibuscunq́ Mundi partibus fuerint, et quocunq́ posthac tempore Vitæ meæ, à me (prædicto Ioanne) per peculiaria illis Dominantia, siue Imperitantia Sancta tua Nomina (hoc itidem libro contenta) fuerint VOCATI, VT citissime ad me (prædictum Ioannem) Veniant: Visibiles, affabiles, placidiq́ mihi appareant: ac mecum, iuxta Voluntatem meam, visibiles morentur: et Vt a me, et ex aspectu meo, per me rogati recedant: ET propter te, et iam quá tibi, in 12. illis Mysticis, supra expressis, Nominibus, debent Reuerentiam et Obedientiam, Vt mihi etiam (Ioanni præfato) amice SATISFACIANT, omni et quocunq́ tempore Vitæ meæ In Omnibus et Singulis, ad eos, Omnes, aliquos, Vel alique eorū) factis Vel faciendis Petitionibus meis, quibuscunq́: Cito, bene, plene, perfecteq́ præstandis perficiendis et complendis, iuxta eorum Virtutes, ac potentias, tam generales, quam proprias, propriaq́ illis a te (O DEVS) iniuncta commissaq́ Officia et Ministeria AMEN.

Per te, IESV CHRISTE.

AMEN

▲
▲ ▲
▲
▲

The Four times Three Names of God (drawn
from the four lines of the Holy Spirit)
Which govern all creatures on earth
(both visible and invisible)
riding with their twelve
standards.

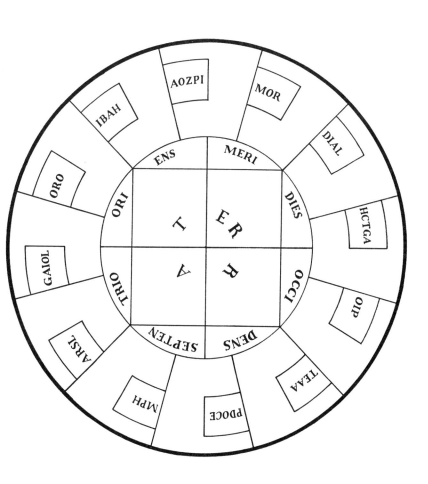

Fundamental Prayer to God and entreaty for the benign
ministry of Good Angels

O IEOVA ZEBAOTH, I invoke and implore most earnestly your Divine Power, Wisdom and Goodness (I, John Dee, your unworthy servant), and most humbly and faithfully ask you to favour and assist me in all my works, words and cogitations, concerning, promoting or procuring your praise, honour and Glory. And by these your twelve mystical names. ORO, IBAH, AOZPI, MOR, DIAL, HCTGA, OIP, TEAA, PDOCE, MPH, ARSL, GAIOL, most ardently do I entreat and implore your Divine and Omnipotent Majesty: that all your faithful Angelic Spirits whose mystical names are expressed in this book and whose offices are briefly noted, in whatever part of the world they be and, in whatever time of my life they are summoned by (the said John) by means of their peculiar powers or authority of your Holy Names (likewise contained in this book), that most swiftly they come to me (the aforesaid John) visible, affable, and appear to me peacefully and remain with me visibly according to my wishes, and that they disappear at my request from me and from my sight. And through you and that reverence and obedience which they owe you in those twelve mystical names above mentioned, that they give satisfaction amicably to me also (the said John), at each and every moment in my life, and in each and every deed or request to all, some or one of them, and to do this quickly, well, completely and perfectly to discharge, perfect and complete all this according to their virtues and power both general and individual and through the injunctions given them by you (O God) and their charged offices and ministry. AMEN.

Through you, Jesus Christ,
AMEN.

*The Names of the Twenty-Four Seniors (referred to
in the Apocalypse of St John) assembled from
the lines of the Father, Son and Holy Spirit:
the gift of these Good Angels is to impart
to Mankind the knowledge and judgement of
human affairs, etc.*

	Name of God BATAIVA, or BATAIVH
East	Abioro, or Habioro
	Aaoxaif
	Htmorda
	Haozpi, or Ahaozpi
	Hipotga
	Autotar

	Name of God ICZHHCA, or ICZHHCL
South	Aidrom, or Laidrom
	Aczinor
	Lzinopo
	Lhctga, or Alhctga
	Lhiansa
	Acmbicu

	Name of God RAAGIOS, or RAAGIOL
West	Srahpm, or Lsrahpm
	Saiinou
	Laoxrp
	Lgaial, or Slgaich
	Ligdisa
	Soaixnt

	Name of God EDLPRNA, or EDLPRNA (*sic*)
North	Aetpio, or AAetpio
	Adoeoet
	Alndood
	Apdoce, or Aapdoce
	Arinnap
	Anodoin

Note

The following Invocation is repeated at each of the Four Quarters: East, South, West and North, changing only the God Names and Seniors as indicated in the above table.

Address to the Six Seniors of the East

O you six Seniors of the East, powerful and faithful ministers of our all-powerful God, in the Name of that God (One and Three) O you (I say) *ABIORO, or HABIORO, AAOZAIF, HTMORDA, HAOZPI, or AHAOZPI, HIPOTGA and AVTOTAR*, through your own divine power and Angelic Name BATAIVA, or BATAIVH, I John Dee, faithful servant of that same God, howsoever conjoined or divided from you, kindly, vehemently and trustfully require and seek that at whatever subsequent occasion I shall wish it during the remainder of my life, all of you or those of you I name (being called, invoked or sought by means of that mystical and Divine Name *BATAIVA or BATAIVH* by me, the aforesaid John) that you be willing to appear to me the said John, visible, affable and content and indeed favourable; that you be willing swiftly, well, truly, plainly, fully and completely to fulfil, execute and complete all my petitions and whatever must be done concerning the knowledge and judgement of human affairs and other matters assigned to your office by God and pertinent to your ministry according to the extent of your virtues, powers, offices and ministry, allowed and committed to you by Omnipotent God. AMEN. Through God's Holy Name *BATAIVA, or BATAIVH*,

AMEN.

(Same address to the six Seniors of the South, West, and North, but with different Names.)

The Names of the Sixteen Good Angels most skilled and effective in Medicine and the cure of sickness: with the Names of the sixteen malevolent ones that can bring sickness.

	Name of God IDOIGO	ARDZA		
East	Czns, or Czons	Xcz	A	O
	Tott, or Toitt	Ato	Z	G
	Sias, or Sigas	Rsi	D	I
	Fmnd, or Fmond	Pfm	R	O
			A	D
				I

	Name of God ANGPOI	VNNAX		
South	Aira, or Aigra	Xai	X	I
	Ormn, or Orpmn	Aor	A	O
	Rsni, or Rsoni	Rrs	N	P
	Iznr, or Izinr	Piz	N	G
			V	N
				A

	Name of God OLGOTA	OALCO		
West	Taco, or Tagco	Mto	O	A
	Nhdd, or Nhodd	Onh	C	T
	Paax, or Patax	Cfa	B	O
	Saiz, or Saaiz	Hsa	A	G
			A	B
				O

	Name of God NOALMR	OLOAG		
North	Opmn, or Opamn	Mop	G	R
	Apst, or Aplst	Oap	A	M
	Scio, or Scmio	Csc	O	I
	Vasg, or Varsg	Hua	L	A
			O	O
				N

(Note: The evil angels have names of three letters, evoked by the reversed God-Names given in the right-hand column.)

Invitation to the Four Good Angels of the East
most skilled and effective in medicine
and the cure of sickness.

O you Four Angels of Light, *Czns, or Czons, Tott, or Toitt, Sias, or Sigas, Fmnd, or Fmond,* potent ministers and disposers of God's medical powers of healing and cures in the eastern part of the world, in the name of the Omnipotent, true and Living God, I John Dee (by His grace, a future citizen of heavenly Jerusalem) vehemently and respectfully seek and require you through the reverence and obedience which you owe to Him our God, and through these His mystical and Divine Names IDOIGO and ARDZA; do earnestly require you both individually and together, to come to me (the aforesaid John) hereafter at whatever moment through the duration of my natural life I should wish it, and willingly to appear content, visible and favourable, perfecting and completing my petitions as swiftly, exactly and perfectly as possible; such requests as I shall seek of all some or each of you by these said Names of God IDOIGO and ARDZA, and which you can most quickly, perfectly, fully and dutifully discharge, complete and fulfil by means of your intrinsic power and strength and the course and method of your peculiar offices or medical duties. AMEN. Through these sacrosanct names of God IDOIGO and ARDZA AMEN.

Note

The same Invocation is employed for the other Quarters – South, West, North – substituting the relevant Names from the above table.

The Names of the Sixteen Good Angels who are
skilled and potent in the discovery, collecting,
use and intrinsic power of metals, and also in
the combining of stones and their powers.

	Name of God LLACZA	PALAM		
East	Oyub, or Oyaub	xoy	M	A
	Paoc, or Pacoc	Apa	A	Z
	Rbnh, or Rbznh	Rrb	L	C
	Diri, or Diari	Pdi	A	A
			P	L
				L

	Name of God ANAEEM	SONDN		
South	Omgg, or Omagg	Xom	N	M
	Gbal, or Gbeal	Agb	D	E
	Rlmu, or Rlemu	Rrl	N	E
	Iahl, or Iamhl	Pia	O	A
			S	N
				A

West	Name of God NELAPR	OMEBB		
	Magm, or Malgm	Mma	B	R
	Leoc, or Leaoc	Ole	B	P
	Vssn, or Vspsn	Cus	E	A
	Ruoi, or Ruroi	Hru	M	L
			O	E
				N

North	Name of God VADALI	OBAVA		
	Gmnm, or Gmdnm	Mgm★	A	I★★
	Ecop, or Ecaop	Oec	V	L
	Amox, or Amlox	Cam	A	A
	Brap, or Briap	Hbr	B	D
			O	A
				V

Address to the Four Good Angels of the East
who are skilled and potent in metals and stones.

O you four Angels of Light, faithful ministers of God (our Maker), you (I say) *Oyvb, or Oyavb, Paoc, or Pacoc, Rbnh, or Rbznh, and Diri, or Diari,* dominant in the eastern part of the world and (through the dispensation of God and his particular gift) most skilled and powerful in the discovery of metals or mineral veins the collecting or accumulation of metallic matter and its use and efficacy, and also in the assembly and power of stones as well as in many other arcane secrets concerning the whereabouts, collecting, nature, properties, efficacy and utilisation of metals and stone: I John Dee, humble and devoted servant of the Omnipotent, living and true God (JEOVA ZEBAOTH himself), through that necessary reverence and obedience which you owe to Him, our God, denoted by those names LLACZA and PALAM do earnestly and confidently require and seek you, both all and singly, to be willing to appear to me (the aforesaid John) benignly, contentedly, visible and affable, at whatever time in the rest of my life I should wish it, that you honour me (the same John) with your favour, and that you be willing most swiftly, visibly, surely, entirely and perfectly to complete and fulfil each and every request which I require all of you, or some, or one, to do or perform. I am content, to be restricted by this condition: that my said petitions,

---

★   Evil angels, or Cacodemons.
★★ Reversed Names of God.

whether totally or for the most part or in some way, involve your particular skill, virtue, potency or faculty (expressed above) in metals or stones, and also that they be required or sought of some or all of you by means of the necessary use of the said Divine Names LLACZA and PALAM by me the aforesaid John: AMEN. Through the said Holy and Mystical names of God LLACZA and PALAM. AMEN.

(The same address is used for the four Angels of the Southern, Western and Northern Quarters, inserting the appropriate names from the above table.)

The Names of the Sixteen Good Angels who are skilled and powerful in Transformation: and also the sixteen manifest names of the malevolent spirits.

	Name of God AIAOAI OIIIT	
East	Abmo, or Abamo	Cab
	Naco, or Naoco	Ona
	Ocnm, or Ocanm	Moc
	Shal, or Shial	Ash

	Name of God CBALPT ARBIZ	
South	Opna, or Opana	Cop
	Doop, or Dolop	Odo
	Rxao, or Rxpao	Mvx
	Axir, or Axtir	Aax

	Name of God MALADI OLAAD	
West	Paco, or Palco	Rpa
	Ndzn, or Ndazn	And
	Iipo, or Iidpo	Xii
	Xrnh, or Xrinh	Exr

	Name of God VOLXDO SIODA	
North	Datt, or Daltt	Rda
	Diom, or Dixom	Adi
	Oopz, or Oodpz	Xoo
	Rgan, or Rgoan	Erg

Address to the Four Good Angels of the East,
skilled and potent in Transformation.

O you Four Good and true Angels of God (our maker) *Abmo, or Abamo, Naco, or Naoco, Ocnm, or Ocanm, and Shal, or Shial,* who are dominant in the eastern part of the world and who have received from our and your Creator a particular power, true knowledge and perfect and absolute potency in transformation in our creation,as it were a gift and office, so that this same true science and perfected power might be imparted and made plain by you to me (preordained by Him) for the Creator's praise, honour and glory. Wherefore I John Dee, the devoted servant of our Creator and God, earnestly desire to promote and amplify His praise, honour and glory, truly, diligently and faithfully among mankind through this your aforementioned knowledge and the true employment of the same. By that God, our maker and by these mystical names of our God which have particular authority and power over you AIAOAI and OIIIT, I strongly require and confidently seek you, individually and together, to be willing to appear to me, the said John, peaceably, content, and visible at whatever point during the remainder of my life and as often as I shall wish; and deigning to appear favourable and friendly to me the said John, that you be willing to fulfil and complete truly, perfectly, plainly, manifestly and fully, all and each of my requests, in whatever manner, that concern and involve your skill in transformations, knowledge and power, such as are required or sought by me, the said John, of one, some or all of you, at whatever subsequent time, through these names of our God set down, AIAOAI and OIIIT; and that you perform and do the same requests at once, without delay or at least as soon as they can be performed in any way. AMEN.

By these Holy and mystical Names of GOD
AIAOAI and OIIIT. AMEN.

(Address to the Four Good Angels of the South, West and North, as above, inserting the appropriate names from the above table.)

The Names of the Sixteen Good Angels that comprehend the species and uses of the living creatures in each of the Four Elements; also expressed are the names of the sixteen cacodaemones.

	Name of God AOVRRZ ALOAI				
East	Acca, or Acuca	Air	Cac	I	Z
	Npat, or Nprat	Water	Onp	A	R
	Otoi, or Otroi	Earth	Mot	O	R
	Pmox, or Pmzox	Fire	Apm	L	V
				A	O
					A

	Name of God SPMNIR LLPIZ				
South	Msal, or Msmal	Air	Cms	Z	R
	Iaba, or Ianba	Water	Oia	I	I
	Izxp, or Izixp	Earth	Miz	P	N
	Stim, or Strim	Fire	Ast	L	M
				L	P
					S

	Name of God IAAASD ATAPA				
West	Xpcn, or Xpacn	Air	Rxp	A	D
	Vasa, or Vaasa	Water	Aua	P	S
	Dapi, or Daspi	Earth	Xda	A	A
	Rnil, or Rnail	Fire	Era	T	A
				A	A
					I

	Name of God RZIONR NRZFM				
North	Adre, or Adire	Air	Rad	M	R
	Sisp, or Siosp	Water	Asi	F	N
	Pali, or Panli	Earth	Xpa	Z	O
	Acar, or Acrar	Fire	Eac	R	I
				N	Z
					R

*Address to the Four Angels of the East, each of
whom understands all the living creatures of one
Element and their uses.*

O you Angels, full of the truth and goodness of God (you I say),
Acca, or Acvca, Npat, or Nprat, Otoi, or Otroi, and Pmox, or Pmzox,
who have authority in the eastern part of the world such that each of
you has your particular gift or office, peculiar skill, knowledge,
power and authority in each of the Four Elements or matrices of the
world. O you ACCA, or ACUCA, eminent Angel that perceives all the
diverse species of living creatures in all the eastern air and perfectly
understands for what uses to mankind they were created by God; you
also illustrious NPAT, or NPRAT, who understands the species and true
use of the living creatures in all the eastern waters; and you famous
OTOI, or OTROI, that exactly comprends the various species that enjoy
life in all the eastern land and for what uses they were created by God;
and finally you PMOX, or PMZOX, shining Angel of God, that has
cognition fully of the vital properties, most secret and efficacious, of
the eastern fire. O you all (I say), faithful ministers of our God and
maker, who, in the eastern part of the world, understand these and
many other secrets and mysteries of the Four Elements, granted,
assigned and deputed to your knowledge and offices by our Omnipotent maker, and are able to impart and clearly communicate such
secrets (with God's approval) to us (called and elected by the living
heavenly voice) to the praise honour and glory of God and through
your own great charity to the human race. Therefore, I John Dee,
most ardent lover and seeker, after secrets of this kind (and that
particularly for the praise, honour and glory of our God) in the name
of that God and our maker, humbly supplicate you that I have
named, both individually and together, trustfully seek and require
you, by the Holy Names of our God AOVRRZ, and ALOAI, willingly
and entirely to fulfil, benignly to grant clearly to enact and lovingly to
accomplish the completion, achievement and execution, both plain,
entire and perfect, of all my requests at whatever occasion in my life
(after this hour) that I should ask and seek the helpful presence and
personal appearance of all or one of you, such petitions as concern
and entail your said particular offices and gifts or your special
knowledge and power, by these Holy Names of God AOVRRZ and
ALOAI, AMEN.

Through these revered and mystical names of God,
AOVRRZ and ALOAI. AMEN.

(Address to the Angels of the other Quarters the same, but with the
names given above.)

The Names of the Sixteen Good Angels that
are skilled and potent in the mixture of natures.

	Name of God ERZLA	
East	Rzla Zlar Larz Arzl	I
	Name of God EBOZA	
South	Boza Ozab Zabo Aboz	A
	Name of God ATAAD	
West	Taad Aadt Adta Dtaa	O
	Name of God ADOPA	
North	Dopa Opad Pado Adop	N★

Address to the Four Good Angels of the East who
are skilful and potent in the mixing of Natures.

O you Four faithful and veracious ministers of Omnipotent God, our Creator *Rzla, Zlar, Larz and Arzl*, who are skilled and powerful in the mixing of natures in the eastern part of the world, I John Dee, devoted servant of Him, our maker, do humbly require and strongly seek you all, and singly, by the Omnipotence of our maker and by the mystical name of our God ERZLA, that at whatever subsequent

★   For the significance of the letters in this column, see Commentary.

moment in my life that I (the aforesaid John) shall call by name, you, or some, or one of you, through the mystical name of our God ERZLA, that you be willing to appear to me (the said John), benign, calm, visible and in person; and gracing me (the said John) with friendship and favour, swiftly, well, fully, plainly and successfully to achieve, acquit and complete all and each of my petitions concerning the mixing of natures and other natural secrets which our maker granted you knowledge of, understanding and power over, as it were for your duties and ministry. AMEN.

Through this Holy and mystical Name of God

ERZLA. AMEN.

(Substitute table names for remaining Quarters)

The Names of the Sixteen Good Angels who are potent in Changing of place.

	Name of God EVTPA	
East	Vtpa Tpau Paut Autp	L
	Name of God EPHRA	
South	Phra Hrap Raph Aphr	A
	Name of God ATDIM	
West	Tdim Dimt Imtd Mtdi	N
	Name of God AANAA	
North	Anaa Naaa Aaan Aana	V

Address to the Four Good Angels of the East
who are potent in changing of place.

O you, faithful and noble Angels and ministers of our Omnipotent Creator, *Vtpa, Tpau, Pavt and Avtp,* that have particular dominion in the eastern part of the world, who are endowed by the Creator with such skill, ability and power that you may truly, quickly, successfully, safely and without any harm, loss or damage to man or thing transported, carry or transfer man or object from one place to another. I John Dee, devoted and humble servant of our maker, all powerful God, through the revered majesty of Him, our maker, and this divine and mystical name EVTPA, do humbly require and ardently request you all and each (before named) that at whatever subsequent time in my life I call you by name or invoke you all, or some of you, or one through God's name, EVTPA, that you appear to me (the said John) benign, favourable, visible and in person, and that you deign to be friendly and favourable to me (the said John); and that you swiftly, well truly, fully and perfectly fulfil, achieve and perfect each and every petition of mine for you to make good concerning local motion or movement from one place to another and other secrets which are committed and ordained to your authority and disposal by our God for His praise, honour and glory. AMEN.

Through the sacred and mystic name of God
EVTPA. AMEN.
(Same address to other quarters substituting names.)

The Names of the Sixteen Good Angels skilled
and potent in Mechanical Arts.

	Name of God HCNBR	
East	Cnbr Nbrc Brcn Rcnb	A
	Name of God HROAN	
South	Roan Oanr Anro Nroa	C

	Name of God PMAGL	
West	Magl Aglm Glma Lmag	M

	Name of God PPSAC	
North	Psac Sacp Acps Cpsa	V

Address to the Four Good Angels of the East skilled
and potent in Mechanical Arts.

Cnbr, Nbrc, Brcn, and Rcnb,[10]

O you four Holy and true ministers of Omnipotent God, our maker, that are granted and given by our God particular ministry in the eastern part of the world in the exercise, imparting, teaching and communication of perfect skill in all Mechanical Arts for the praise honour and glory of our God. I, John Dee, baptised and inscribed servant of our God and desiring to serve Him faithfully, wisely and strongly (to the benefit and solace of the Good and Elect and to the shame and confusion of the wicked, enemies of our Omnipotent God) do humbly request and vehemently seek you all (before named), through the Omnipotent wisdom of God, our maker, and through his sacred and mystical name HCNBR, to straightway appear and be present, benign, peaceable, in person and visible to me (the said John) at whatever subsequent moment of my life I (the said John) should call or invoke you all, or some or one of you by name; and that besides be willing to be kind and favourable to me; and that you achieve, complete and fulfil, truly, fully, plainly and entirely each and all of my requests to some or one of you, concerning any Mechanical Art, any conclusion or Mechanical experiment. AMEN.

Through the mystic name of God, HCNBR. AMEN.

(Address to the Angels of the other Quarters the same, inserting appropriate table names.)

Names of the Sixteen Good Angels, skilled and potent in understanding the secrets of all men.

	Name of God HXGZD	
East	Xgzd Gzdx Zdxg Dxgz	A

	Name of God HIAOM	
South	Iaom Aomi Omia Miao	S

	Name of God PNLRX	
West	Nlrx Lrxn Rxnl Xnlr	I

	Name of God PZIZA	
North	Ziza Izaz Zazi Aziz	R

Address to the Four Good Angels of the East, skilled and potent in understanding the secrets of all men.

O you, Four wise and veracious Angels and ministers of Omnipotent God, our maker, you (I say) *Xgzd, Gzdx, Zdxg, and Dxgz*, honoured with the great and especial gift and office from our God in the secrets of men in the eastern part of the world their understanding and full comprehension. I, John Dee, devoted servant of God, induced by no curiosity, nor solicitous inquisition after the state of other men, their secrets, inclinations, actions, circumstances, good or evil deeds (unless it be in some way useful or necessary, or can be so, in part or whole, to the Christian republic for such things to be known, discovered or understood by me (the said John)). I, (the aforesaid John), through God's omniscience and His mystic name, HXGZD, humbly require and vehemently seek of you, above named, both all and each, that at whatsoever subsequent moment of my life, I should call or invoke all, or some, or each of you through the above name of God, HXGZD, you should immediately appear to me, benignly and placidly; be present in person and visible, and acquit, fulfil and perfect each and every one of my petitions (to some or all of you) concerning the Secrets, state, and condition of any man, swiftly, truly, fully and entirely. AMEN.

Through God's sacred and mystic name,

HXGZD. AMEN.

(*Address to the Four Angels of the remaining Quarters the same, inserting the appropriate names from the above table.*)

★

★ ★ ★

★

★

★

Notes

1 From a signature in Sloane MS. 3191, I believe this to have been Robert Jones.
2 Ibid., Susanna Jones.
3 For a fuller account of this matter see Elias Ashmole's flyleaf note to *Liber Mysteriorum* I–V (Sloane MS. 3188, British Museum) or the published version in my *Heptarchia Mystica of John Dee*, pp. 18–19.
4 From the Latin:
'48 *Claves Angelicae, Ao 1584:*
Cracovie, ab, Aprilus 13,
ad Julii 13, (diversis temporibus) Recepte:
ex mera Dei nostri:
Misericordia:
Cui Soli, omnis Laus, Honor, et Gloria, Amen. Liber 18.'
5 From the Latin: '*Liber Scientiae, Auxilii, et Victoriae Terrestris, Ao 1585 Maij 2o (stylo novo) Cracoviae in Polonia.*'
6 From the Latin:
   I: *Nonaginta et vnius partium series continua.*
  II: *91 Partium Terrae nomina ab Hominibus imposita.*
 III: *91 Partium Terrae nomina Divinitus imposita.*
 IV: *91 Divinae Impositionis Characteres symmetrici.*
  V: *30 Bonorum Principum Aereorum ordines sphaerici.*
 VI: *Bonorum Ministrorum vniuscuius & Ordinis Numerrus Tripartitus.*
VII: *Bonorum Ministrorum in singulis Ordinibus Tripartitorum, Numeri Totales.*

VIII: *12 Angeli Reges ipsis 30 Ordinibus praedominantes. qui 12 etiam Tribuum praesides sunt.*
  IX: *12 Tribus Populi Israelitici, in Dispersione.*
   X: *4 Plagae Mundi Tribubus Dispersis assignatae.*

7   From the Latin:
Quando diuidebat Altissimus Gentes Quando
separabat filios ADAM, constituit terminos
populorum, iuxta numerum filiorum Israel.

Moyses, in Cantico: Deuter. 32

8   Et habebat murum magnum, et altum, habentem
portas Duodecim: et in portis, ANGELOS
Duodecim, et Nomina inscripta, quae sunt
Nomina Duodecim Tribuum filiorum Israel.

Apocalypseos: Cap. 24.

9   As the original manuscript lacks a title page, I have used that given by Elias Ashmole in his *Catalogue of such of Dr Dee's MSS. as are come in my hands* (Ashmole MSS. No. 1790, fol. 52R). R. T.

10   In this Invocation Dee records the names of the Four Good Angels in this position, probably as an afterthought.

III
Commentaries on the Angelic Manuscripts of John Dee

1. The Forty-Eight Angelic Keys

From the outset, these calls or Keys will be seen to bear striking resemblance to the cryptical utterances of the Apocalypse. References to 'the vials of wrath'[1] (9th Key), 'the bed of a Harlot (Jezebel?)' (19th Key), 'the house of death (Babylon)' (9th Key), 'sharp sickles' (3rd Key), cries of 'Woe unto the earth' and many other elements, strongly indicate Apocalyptic influence. Although it cannot be stated with any degree of certainty, it is my personal view that Kelly was to some measure 'inspired' by passages in the *Book of Revelation*, and subconsciously coloured the Angelic invocations.

The Forty-eight Keys comprise eighteen lesser invocations and the Key or Call of the Thirty Aires or Aethers. For each of the Aires, the same Key is repeated varying the name of the Aire (Lil, Arm, Zom, etc.) in each instance when recited in the Angelic language, and the number (1st, 2nd, 3rd, Aire) when read in English. Dee and Kelly are further instructed, that the Keys are in fact forty-nine as a hidden call 'that of the Godhead and not to be called' is mystically represented. The Forty-eight Keys were intended to be used, together with the Holy Table and Sigillum Aemeth, to bring about great changes in the world and a new 'state of perfection' in all things.

There is no evidence to indicate that Dee ever made practical use of the Forty-eight Keys, which seem to stand apart from the other elements of the Angelic magic, despite the titanic efforts of Mathers and others to interrelate the calls with the Angelic Tablets and other aspects of Dee's work. With the Dee papers the word 'system' must be used lightly.

It has been suggested (in some depth) that Dee's record of Enochian magic is in reality a system of encipherment which he employed in his role as the 'Queen's intelligencer'. It is well known that Dee was deeply concerned with matters of state security (Dee invented the title 'British Empire'), and possessed an extensive knowledge of encoding and decoding messages. To this end he was overjoyed when he discovered a manuscript copy of the *Stenographia* of Trithemius (teacher of Cornelius Agrippa) which disguises a

system of encipherment under the mask of a magical text. Of the
Stenographia Dee writes: 'a boke for which many a learned man has
long sought and dayly doth seeke; whose use is greater than the fame
thereof is spread'.

In modern times the chief exponent of the 'cipher theory' has been
Richard Deacon. In his book *John Dee: Scientist, Geographer, Astrologer and Secret Agent to Elizabeth I*,[2] Richard Deacon sets forth a mass
of material to validify his case. How far he succeeds is, to a certain
degree, a matter of conjecture. However, it is my opinion that
Deacon's work does contribute a possible solution to *some* of the
more enigmatic aspects of Dee's magic and his angle of approach is
well worth investigating in further depth. The situation may well be
as D. P. Walker suggests[3] in his analysis of the *Stenographia* of
Trithemius, that Dee's Invocations can be read on two levels, one as a
treatise on Angel-magic, and the other – hidden beneath the plain-
text – a system of cryptography.

The above may be seen by some readers to be a retraction of my
earlier ideas regarding Dee's magic (cf. *The Heptarchia Mystica of John
Dee*), but I forward my present view in the light of recent research
undertaken by my colleagues and myself. It has even been indicated
that elements in the Angelic language may have been inspired by
Dee's delvings into ancient Welsh (another link with Cati?). Finally,
when one considers John Dee's sentiments towards the sixteenth-
century Spanish throne, consider the Angelic word for iniquity:
'*madrid*'.

2. The Book of Knowledge, Help and Earthly Victory

In this manuscript Dee tabulates the correspondences of the Thirty-
Aires, or Aethers. First he lists ninety-one regions of the earth 'named
by man': and then adds a series of divinely imposed equivalent titles;
symmetrical characters; details of the associated Angelic Hosts;
Angelic Kings and their relevant Hebrew tribes and finally, the
assignation of the twelve tribes of Israel at their dispersion.

Regarding the reception of this information Dee records (in his
Seventh Book of the Mysteries) on 23 May 1584:

> (E. K.) There appeareth a great thing like a Globe, turning upon
> two axell-trees (marginal note: *D: The earthly Globe appearing*).
> Nalvage [the Angel]: Turn to the first Air . . . (D) I have done.
> Nalvage: The Earth in the first ayre, is this [E. K. pointing on
> that Globe to it.]
> D. We beseech you to bound or determine the Countries or
> Portions of the Earth, by their uttermost Longitudes and
> Latitudes, or by some other certain manner.

Nal. Our manner is, not as it is for worldlings: We determine not places after the forms of legs, or as leaves are: neither we can imagin any thing after the fashion of an [D] horn: as those that are Cosmographer do.

Notwithstanding the Angel of the Lord appeared unto Ptolomie, and opened unto him the parts of the Earth: but some he was commanded to secret: and those are Northward under your Pole. But to you, the very true names of the world in her Creation are delivered.

D. There appeared a great water, long and narrow, reddish, and thereby appeared . . . written *Egypt*.[4]

These Ptolemaic divisions of the earth are referred to in Cornelius Agrippa's *First Book of Occult Philosophy*, Chapter 31, entitled *How Provinces, and Kingdoms are Distributed to Planets*. Of these Agrippa states:

> These we have in this manner, gathered from Ptolomey's opinion to which according to the writings of other Astrologers, many more may be added. But he who knows how to compare these divisions of provinces according to the Divisions of the Stars, with the Ministry of the Ruling Intelligences, and Blessings of the Tribes of Israel, the lots of the Apostles, and Typical Seals of the Sacred Scripture, shall be able to obtain great and prophetical oracles, concerning every region of things to come.[5]

Dee's list of earthly zones (with certain Angelically derived exceptions), follows Agrippa in general, but gives a different order of place names, and makes no reference to planetary attributions.

Of the extent and dominion of the Aires, or Aethers the Angel Nalvage states: 'Understand therefore, that from the *fire* to the *earth*, there are thirty places or abidings: one above and beneath another: wherein these aforesaid Creatures have their aboad, for a time.'[6]

This spacial allocation of the Aethers was perfectly in line with the pre-Copernican model of the universe generally accepted in Dee's time (although Dee was one of the first open advocates of the true, sun-centred, Copernican system).

This system placed the Earth at the centre, being in itself the first of the four Elements of Aristotelian physics, surrounded with the spheres of Water, Air and Fire. Above these elemental regions revolved the spheres of the Moon, Mercury, Venus, the Sun, Mars, Jupiter, Saturn, the 'fixed stars' and the *Primum Mobile*. Therefore, the thirty areas of space occupied by the Aethers were confined to the Elemental zones related to the Earth. As the Angels of the Aethers are held to '. . . bring in and again dispose of Kings and all the Governements upon Earth, and vary the Natures of things: with the variation of every moment',[7] their region once more reflects the Aristotelian conception that change could only take place beneath the sphere of the Moon.

The Angels imply that the 'New Era', or 'State of Perfection' that Dee so earnestly desired, was to be established by the invocation and manipulation of powers of the Aethers: 'Unto whom, the providence of the eternal Judgement, is already opened.'[8]

Note

1. In my transcription of this manuscript I have rendered the names of the Twelve Tribes of Israel into their modern forms: Judah, Zebulun, Simeon, Reuben, Gad, Manasseh, Ephraim, Benjamin, Asher, Dan, Naphtali and Issachar. Dee employs: Jehudah, Zabulon, Simeon, Ruben, Gad, Manasse, Ephraim, Benjamin, Asseir, Dan, Nephthalim and Isacaraah.
2. It is to be noted that the first symmetrical character in Dee's manuscript is different, in form, to that given in his combined table of characters (Figure 10). The reason for this difference is unknown.
3. For further information on the physical location of the Ninety-one divisions of the earth, see Appendix C.

3. A Book of Supplications and Invocations

This book begins with a series of three square tables and one round table. The first table, although containing all relevant elements of the second, proves to be erroneous and Dee includes a note to this effect: 'On 20th April, 1587, these reformed by Raphael.' The second table (Figure 9) provides a basis from which a number of God and Angelic names are subsequently drawn in accordance with certain rules.

The Table as a whole consists of four lesser tables, or tablets joined together by a central cross: The Cross of Union. Although each lesser table is treated independently, the same rules of construction apply to the involved names.

As Dee tabulates the entire system of these names in his *Book of Supplications and Invocations*, a brief example will serve to illustrate their method of construction:

(a) First the Three Names of God are drawn from the 'Line of the Holy Spirit' (Linea Spiritus Sancti): ORO, IBAH, AOZPI. This is the central line in the table, numbered 1 in the diagram.

EASTERN TABLE

2

```
  r Z i l a f A y t l p a
  a r d Z a i d p a L a m
  c z o n s a r o Y a v b
  T o i T t z o P a c o C
  S i g a s o m r b z n h
  f m o n d a T d i a r i
1 o r o i b A h a o z p i
  t N a b v V i x g a s d
  O i i i t T p a l O a i
  A b a m o o o a C u c a
  N a o c O T t n p r n T
  o c a n m a g o t r o i
  S h i a p r a p m z o x
```

(b) Second a further God Name is generated from the seven letters at the centre of the equal-armed Cross formed by the intersection of the Line of the Holy Spirit and the double column of letters known as 'The Line of the Father and the Son' (Linea, Patris, Filiique), numbered 2 in the above diagram: BATAIVA (or BATAIVH, depending on what final letter is employed) viz:

2

a T

l b A H a

V i

(*Note*: letters form a clockwise spiral)

(c) Third, the six names of the Seniors are drawn from the equal-armed cross as follows:

```
                    f A
                    i d
                    a r
                    z o
                    o m
                    a T
        o r o i b A H a o z p i
                    V i
                    T p
                    o o
                    T t
                    a g
                    r a
```

(H)ABIORO, AAOZAIF, HTMORDA, (A)HAOZPI, HIPOTGA, AUTOTAR, read from the centre of the cross outwards.

(d) Fourth, eight further God Names are formed from the letters which form calvary crosses in the lesser quarters of each square. The first name taken from the vertical line of the cross and read downwards, is held to call forth the spirits. The second name, taken from the horizontal line of each cross, is held to command the spirits, e.g.:

```
                    i
        a   r   d   z   a
                    o
                    i
                    g
                    o
```

(*Upper left-hand quarter of the Eastern Table*)
IDOIGO: To call forth.
ARDZA: To command.

(e) The names of the sixteen Angels which answer to the God Names taken from the calvary crosses, are formed from the four lines of letters that fall beneath the horizontal God Name on each cross. Depending on the use of the central letter, they are of four, or five characters. Those under the power of Idoigo, Ardza are therefore:

$$Cz(o)ns$$
$$To(i)tt$$
$$Si(g)as$$
$$Fm(o)nd$$

To these a series of further Angelic names are added, constructed from the permutations of the names given *above* each calvary cross. These names are in turn answerable to God Names derived in the following manner:

The letters contained in the Cross of Union are formed into a 5×4 square thus:

E	X	A	R	P
H	C	O	M	A
N	A	N	T	A
B	I	T	O	M

By prefixing the appropriate letter from the square (or table of union) expanded God Names are produced, e.g. the E of exarp added to the name of four letters found above the cross of Idoigo-Ardza (RZLA) produces ERZLA, the Name of God that has power over the four Angels Rzla, Zlar, Larz, Arzl, the permutations of the name Rzla. Similarly the remaining letters of the line e--x,a,r,p are added to the first two letters of the Angelic names beneath the cross to produce their demonic counterparts:

$$Xcz$$
$$Ato$$
$$Rsi$$
$$Pfm$$

which are called forth and commanded by the reversed names of God. The same rules apply throughout the system.
(*When conducting these permutations, Dee identifies the lesser square in question by annexing the unused upper letter in a given calvary cross to his tabulations.*)

The third square table given at the beginning of the *Book of Supplications*, contains the symmetrical characters of *The Book of*

Knowledge, Help and Earthly Victory and forges a possible link between the two manuscripts.

The round table bears the twelve names of God extracted from the squares but, strangely (possibly a transcription error), transposes the names applied to the north and west quarters.

The formula of the *Book of Supplications and Invocations* was derived from a vision which appeared to Edward Kelly on the morning of 20 June 1584:

> There appeared to him (E.K.) four very fair Castles, standing in the four parts of the world: out of each he heard the sound of a trumpet.
>
> Then seemed out of every Castle a cloath to be thrown on the ground, of more then the breadth of a Table-cloath.
>
> Out of that in the East, the cloath seemed to be red, which was cast.
>
> Out of that in the South, the cloath seemed white.
>
> Out of that in the West, the cloath seemed green, with great knops on it.
>
> Out of that in the North, spread, or thrown out from the gate underfoot, the cloath seemed to be very black.
>
> Out of every gate then issued one Trumpeter, whose Trumpets were of strange form, wreathed, and growing bigger and bigger toward the end.
>
> After the Trumpeter followed three Ensign bearers.
>
> After them six ancient men, with white beards and staves in their hands.
>
> Then followed a comely man, with very much Apparel on his back, his Robe having a long train.
>
> Then followed one great Crosse, and about that four lesser Crosses.
>
> These Crosses had on them, each of them ten, like men, their faces distinctly appearing on the four parts of the Crosses, all over.
>
> After the Crosses followed 16 white Creatures.
>
> And after them, an infinite number seemed to issue, and spread themselves orderly in a compasse, almost before the four foresaid Castles.

Dee later engraved the vision on a plate of gold in honour of its reception: preserved to this day in the collection of the British Museum (see Appendix B for diagram). It is interesting to note that a manuscript (Sloane MS. 307), written at least a century after Dee's death, contains copious notes on the methods by which the Angelic names are drawn from the squares, together with rules for their practical application. A part copy of the same manuscript circulated in the Hermetic Order of the Golden Dawn under the title 'Document H, CLAVICULA TABULARUM ENOCHI'.[9]

Notes

1 In the ninth Enochian Key 'eight vials of wrath' are referred to. The Apocalypse (Chap. XV, XVI) mentions only seven. They are the seven golden cups, or vessels 'full of the wrath of God' that the Angels poured out upon the earth, and not, as Geoffrey James suggests in his *Enochian Evocation*, an early form of violin!

2 *John Dee, Scientist, Geographer, Astrologer and Secret Agent to Elizabeth I*, Richard Deacon, Frederick Muller, London, 1968.

3 *Spiritual and Demonic Magic*, D. P. Walker, London, 1975.

4 See *A True and Faithful Relation*, p. 153.

5 *Three Books of Occult Philosophy*, Henry Cornelius Agrippa, Chthonios Books, London, 1987, p. 62, Book I.

6 *A True and Faithful Relation*, p. 140.

7 *Ibid.*

8 *Ibid.*

9 My copy of this document (reproduced from the collection of the late Gerald Yorke) contains the note:
'The following is copied from a note in the hand of W. Wynn Westcott in the back of an MS. copy of Flying Roll XVI in the possession of G. M. Watkins, bookseller –

> Title page of Ritual H. (Enochian System)
> English title letter – H
> > Clavicula
> > Tabularum   (Key of the Enochian Tables)
> > Enochi

A MS. escaped from the Rituals of Ordinis Ros. Rub. et Aur.
Tablet Letters corrected and alterations added 1891

> Authorised by G. H. Soror Sap Dom Ast
> > The property of
> > V. H. Fra. Sapere Aude,
> > The Registrar of the Second Order.

Aug. 1888.

5o = 6o Taken from the Notebook of F. L. Gardner.

Dated 5 June 1895.

A note in Golden Dawn cypher states 'Sloane MS. 307'.

Bulfinch del.   Godfrey Sc.

DR SIMON FORMAN,

ASTROLOGER.

Engraved from the Original Drawing

in the Collection of the Right Honble

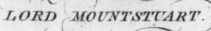

LORD MOUNTSTUART.

Publish'd July 1.1776 by F. Blyth No.87. Cornhill.

SIMON FORMAN   *Courtesy British Library Board*

IV
Simon Forman
Physician, Astrologer and Necromancer
1552 – 1611

These metaphysics of magicians
And necromantic books are heavenly;
Lines, circles, letters and characters,
Ay, these are those that Faustus most desires.

Dr Faustus, C. Marlowe

Born under the Sign of the Goat (30 December), in 1552, at the Wiltshire village of Quidhampton, Simon Forman entered a Tudor world poised on the brink of uncertainty. The young King Edward's health was rapidly failing (he died of tuberculosis on 6 July 1553), and many feared the consequences of Mary's succession: as history records, this was not without considerable justification.

Had fate allowed Mary more than five short bloody years to pursue her relentless persecution of all that she considered heretical, a very different Simon Forman may have emerged. For during his life Forman was to become notorious as a necromancer: expert in the arts of conjuring spirits; communication with the dead; and the manufacture of philtres; charms and talismans; aphrodisiacs and even poisons. In high places his trusted – and perhaps, feared – reputation was to earn him the title 'sweet Father Forman'.

As the details of Simon's earlier life have been adequately dealt with elsewhere[1] we need not elaborate here, though it is worth mentioning that, like Dee, he received a grammar-school education, and became reasonably proficient in Latin.

In 1589 (at the age of 37) Simon moved to London where he took lodgings near Cripplegate. Although his establishment in the city first led to an empty purse and its attendant hardship; affairs quickly took a turn for the better when he became actively engaged in the practice of magic and astrology, and later, medicine.

London provided the ideal outlet for Simon's various talents. A city of complexities, problems, poverty, riches, and innumerable maladies of the flesh; it was ripe for the picking.

Simon's medical qualifications remain a subject of some speculation. It seems that it was not until 1603 that he received an official licence (from Cambridge University) to exercise his art, and before this he was constantly harassed by the Guild of Barber-Surgeons and the Royal College of Physicians for his 'illicit' ministrations.

For the most part it seems that Simon chose to ignore the admonishments of the authorities, and although this was finally to lead to his imprisonment (for a year) and a hefty fine, he remained undeterred and escaped beyond their jurisdiction to Lambeth.

To Forman's credit he behaved with great courage during the frequent visitations of plague that vexed the city. While many doctors fled to the country to avoid the pestilence, Forman remained in town, along with other valiant souls, to administer to the afflicted. His cures, crude as they were, were not totally without success; he even suggested that the rats that infested London were somehow responsible – could he have guessed that the rat-flea passed on the bacillus? A short, yet unlikely, step before the invention of the microscope.

In addition to the usual diagnostic techniques of urinology, physiognomy and haematology, Forman utilised astrological calculations in order to assess his patients' condition. His curative measures involved the use of herbal remedies, minerals, lancing, bleeding, and possibly the application of leeches. None of this was unusual in Elizabethan times when doctors employed poultices of cow dung and unguents compounded of lizards and snakes' vertebrae. But Simon seemed to succeed where others failed and soon he amassed a considerable fortune (at his death his estate was valued at £1,200, a very substantial sum by seventeenth-century standards).

Aside from his, what can only be termed, obsession with magic and astrology, Forman possessed a voracious sexual appetite. His copious diaries teem with amorous escapades, all, I might add, of a highly heterosexual nature. In the diaries the term *halek* is used to denote the act of sexual intercourse. Judging by the frequency of its usage, in reference to his wife and several mistresses, we are left in no doubt regarding the status of Simon's virility. Freudian elements often entered his dreams and in one which he records during January 1597, he even extends his passion to the Virgin Queen, Elizabeth:

> I dreamt that I was with the Queen, and that she was a little elderly woman in a coarse white petticoat all unready; and she and I walked up and down through lanes and closes, talking and reasoning of many matters. At last we came over a great close where were many people, and there were two men at hard words. One of them was a weaver, a tall man with a reddish beard, distract of his wits. She talked to him and he spoke very merrily unto her, and at last did take her and kiss her. So I took

her by the arm and put her away; and told her the fellow was
frantic. And so we went from him and I led her by the arm still
and then we went through a dirty lane. She had a long white
smock, very clean and fair, and it trailed in the dirt and her coat
behind. I took her coat and did carry it up a good way, and then
it hung too low before. I told her she could do me a favour to let
me wait on her, and she said I should. Then, said I: 'I mean to
wait *upon* you and not under you, that I might make this belly a
little biger to carry up this smock and coats out of the dirt.' And
so we talked merrily and then she began to lean upon me, when
we were past the dirt, and to be very familiar with me, and
methought she began to love me. And when we were alone, out
of sight, methought she would have kissed me.[2]

As the Queen deliberately cultivated an image of Virgin purity and
unobtainable female sexuality, perhaps such dreams were not uncommon amongst her male subjects.

Although many scandalous accusations were directed towards
Forman during his lifetime, the incident which historically brands
him as a nefarious necromancer and poisoner, reached its conclusion
some years after his death.

The beautiful young Countess of Somerset (formerly Frances
Essex, daughter of the Earl of Suffolk) was unhappy in her arranged
marriage to the Earl of Essex, and employed philtres supplied by
Forman in an attempt to render her husband impotent. She apparently succeeded and, as the marriage remained unconsummated, a
decree of nullity was subsequently granted.

Having gained her freedom from Essex, the young lady proceeded
to make amorous overtures to the Earl of Somerset whom she had
long desired. It is said that she secured the Earl's love by image-magic
involving waxen figures constructed by her 'sweet father', Forman.
Once more her ardent wish was granted and she married Somerset in
1613. The Earl's friend Sir Thomas Overbury had, it seemed, tried to
warn Somerset of his new wife's involvement with Forman, but
before he could get word to the Earl he was arrested under some
political charge and imprisoned in the Tower of London.

The Countess, being aware of Overbury's intentions, seized the
opportunity afforded by his imprisonment and made plans to poison
him. As Forman was dead, a former associate of his was summoned:
Mrs Anne Turner, a skilled poisoner. It seems that Mrs Turner was
prevailed upon to secrete toxic substances in Overbury's food, and
shortly afterwards he was found dead in his cell.

Anne Turner was accused of murdering Overbury, and after she
gave her account, the Countess and Earl were also arrested as

accomplices. They were tried by Lord Chief Justice, Sir Edward Coke in 1616, who on hearing of the earlier sorceries, denounced Forman as the Devil, and Anne Turner as his daughter.

All three were found guilty, but the Earl and his wife were finally pardoned by King James. Anne Turner was put to death at Tyburn.

Forman's diary records that he met with John Dee on 26 July 1604 at the House of a certain 'Mr Staper'. Although in many ways their common interest in the spirit world and astrology would seem to weld them together as kindred magicians, their practical techniques differ greatly. Dee always approached his Angelic operations from a devotional angle employing, as we have seen, prayer and pious ejaculations as his chief method of invocating the spirits; whereas Forman, like Kelly, was much given to the grimoire approach advocated by such works as *The Key of Solomon* and the *Pseudomarchia* of John Weyer (Johannes Wierus).

Evidence of Forman's somewhat 'fleshy' attitude towards the Mysteries is contained in a manuscript[3] that once belonged to the celebrated Dr John Caius.[4]

If the date on this manuscript is to be believed – 1558 – it cannot of course be Forman's own work – he was six years old – but as it seems to be in his hand, it is most likely a transcript of an earlier work that came into his possession.

The content of the manuscript is of great interest. It proves to be a type of practical guide to magical operations set out as a beginner's instructional manual. It lists the colours of the inks used in drawing characters and talismans; the order in which the spirits are to be called forth; perfumes; protective seals, and details of planetary hours together with a mass of other related material. It is without doubt that Simon made use of such manuscripts in his frequent encounters with the spirit world which prompted such diary entries as:

> He cast out much fire, and kept a wonderful ado; but we could not bring him to human form: he was seen like a great black dog and troubled the folk in the house much and feared them. And between 11 and 12 at night the bed (shook?) four or five times, and cast out such fire and brimstone that it stank mightily. That night he kept much ado and reared mightily.

This spirit was called on the Eve of All Hallows' 1597. He was to return on All Souls' day following:

> This night he came according to his wont and raved much; we bound him strongly and kept him till almost four o'clock in the morning.

The shape-changing, binding and the general ferocity of the spirit are all indicative of the ceremonial magic of the grimoires. A far cry from the docile Angel magic of John Dee.

Although many notes and tracts belonging to Forman have survived, it remains uncertain which formal magical texts he utilised in his various necromantic experiments. To bridge this gap I have been at pains to discover a hitherto unpublished manuscript typical in form and representative of Forman's Age. To this end I have reproduced an English text which I came across while attempting to catalogue the most important magical tracts in the British Museum collection.[5]

The English manuscript, anonymous; of uncertain date; and mysterious origin; suited my purpose admirably. In addition it forges a tenuous link with Dee's Angel magic, in as much that it makes mention of *Liber Scientiae Terrestris*; the book of the Thirty Aires, reproduced elsewhere in this volume.

The 'grimoire' lacks a title page but the first folio proclaims it to be an *Operation by the Regal Spirit Usiel*, by means of which twenty-eight further spirits (of the day and night) may be called.

OPERATION BY THE REGAL SPIRIT USIEL

THE GREAT SEAL
OF KING USIEL

THE LESSER SEAL
ACCORDING TO TRITHEMEUS

The Spirit Usiel is a great and potent King, and third in Degree and Order under ye mighty Spirit Amenadiel Emperor of the West Angle of the Air; and hath his Mansion in the North-West point of the compass, wherein he ruleth over many other Spiritual Princes and Dukes with many other Servient and Subservient Spirits residing in the said Mansion.

This Regal Spirit Usiel hath many Spiritual Dukes attending him in the day and many in the night and who again have many servient and subservient Spirits in Degree, Order, and Office, superiour and inferiour serving under them. The Diurnal Spirits (or Spirits of the day) may be moved and called forth to visible appearance in the day; and the Nocturnal Spirits (or Spirits of the night) may be moved and called forth in the night, for the Diurnal Spirits appear not in the night, nor the Nocturnal in the Day.

Out of the many fore mentioned Spiritual Dukes and Presidential Spirits serving in Degree, Order, and Office under Usiel we shall nominate only fourteen Diurnal Dukes and fourteen Nocturnal with their proper Seals or characters appropriated unto each of them and also a particular number of servient and subservient attending them viz:

DIURNAL DUKES

14

1 Abazia		40★	8 Maqui		40
2 Ameta		40	9 Amandiel		40
3 Arnen		40	10 Barsu		30
4 Herne		40	11 Ganaeu		30
5 Saefir		40	12 Hissam		30
6 Poziel		40	13 Tabariel		30
7 Saefaz		40	14 Usiniel		30

*Numbers in this column refer to the servient spirits. R.T.

NOCTURNAL DUKES

14

1 Ansoel		40	8 Adan		40
2 Godiel		40	9 Asuriel		20
3 Barfos		40	10 Almoel		20
4 Burfa		40	11 Pathyr		20
5 Saddiel		40	12 Marae		20
6 Sobiel		40	13 Laspharō		10
7 Ossidiel		40	14 Ethiel		10

The Superiour Spirits of this (first) Order or Mansion are by nature courteous, benevolent and Obediant, and although they have many servants yet they seldom bring any visibly with them, except when requested, or upon official occasion. Yet, notwithstanding the servient Spirits may be made use of by reason are they superiour and servient Spirits of this Mansion and according to their degree, nature, Order, and Office subjected and constrain by ye influence power and force of invocation comanding, calling forth and moving to visible appearance and obedience.

The Office of ye Spirits of this (second) Mansion is to reveal, declare and shew forth upon demand ye very truth and certainty of hidden treasure and of all such wayes and means that may conduce, to ye discovery finding and obtaining ye same, and yet no other Spirits of any Order, office or Mansion whatsoever, or other wandering powers out of Mansion or place of recidence, unto whome by Nature and office ye charge herein may be said to be referred to be so powerful in the discovery and delivering thereof as those of this Mansion and Order have, besides those elsewhere shewed forth and treated in Liber Scientiae Terrestris – etc.

The haveing [a] place convenient, prepared and well befitting this purpose, turning thy self in Action and Operation towards ye North West pouynt of ye compass, with zelous devotion, undaunted resolusion and great eagerness and earnestness of spirit, distincly Reherse, read, or say the following Ivocations:

O Thou great Creator, of heaven and Earth and of all things under ye heavens, ye God to Whose comand and Power are subjected, all Spiritual and temporal Creatures and to ye Glory of our God, ye Cherubims and Serapfins, with numberless Saints, and angels sing eternal haleluyahs. O glorieuse majesty to whom all this and more honour can be expressed, [and] due. We humbly desire in and by ye Mercies of our blessed Savior, great God thy blesseing and protection in all things and next to which may relate to our souls Thy immediett power in all that may be necessary to perfect this our present Operation, whether it is or may be in any of us want of faith wisdome or power, O Lord assist us there with, or if there be anything which wee do not rightly understand, illuminate our understanding, that wee not only in this but in all other of they wonders and marvles may be more ready to give thanks for and praise Thy great Name Jehovah, O Lord let Thy Spirit be with us, in ye carring on and finishing thereof, preserve and defend us both now and for ever more from ye malice and envye of ye Spirits of darkness, enemies of mankind suffor them not we beseech Thee to breed discord or discention amongst us, but have mercy upon us protect us and let our cry come unto Thee. Grant our petitions, O Lord who are not worthy of ye leste of Thy mercies, cause those Sublunar Spirits which we have and are now by they permission intend to invocate to obey our Invocations and Imediately appear-before us to aid and assist us subject them to us, direct us and guide us, let prosperity in all, but esspecialy in this, attend us and if of Thy mercy thou art pleased to grant our desires, grant that we may not be exalted with pride in attributing the least of this to our power, but Ye wee humbly acknowledge it to be thine own abundant mercy to whose honour and glory wee unanimously desire to sing, Eternal praisse amen, amen, amen, etc.

Note

Following the above, the manuscript continues with a series of conjurations similar in nature to those found in the *Key of Solomon*, and concludes with the usual dismissal of the Spirits, or Licence to Depart.

Postscript

On 8 September 1611 Simon Forman died. According to an account by William Lilly, Forman had astrologically predicted his final hour with perfect accuracy, and on that fated day, while rowing on the Thames (towards Puddle-dock), he fell dead at the oars.

Midnight sounds, and the great Christ Church bell
And many a lesser bell sound through the room,
And it is All Souls night. . .

A ghost may come. . .

Notes

1   *The Case Books of Simon Forman*, A. L. Rowse, Weidenfeld & Nicolson, 1974. Also *Autobiography and Personal Diaries of Dr Simon Forman, the Celebrated Astrologer*, ed. James O. Halliwell, London, 1849.
2   Ashmole MSS. 226; see also *Elizabeth I*, P. Johnson, p. 117; *The Case Books of Simon Forman*, A. L. Rowse, p. 31; *The Elizabethan Renaissance*, Rowse, p. 144.
3   Add. MS. 36,674 British Library.
4   John Caius, or Kay (1510–1573), scholar and physician to Edward VI and Mary. The Forman manuscript and certain other items were probably bound up in this volume at a later date.
5   Treatise contained in Sloane MS. 3702 BL.

ROBERT FLUDD *Courtesy The Wellcome Institute*

V
Robert Fludd
Hermetic Philosopher and Medical Practitioner 1574–1637

Little is known regarding the earlier life of Robert Fludd. He was born in 1574 at Milgate House, Bearsted (near Maidstone), Kent, the fifth son of Sir Thomas Fludd, Treasurer for Her Majesty's forces in the Netherlands. Apart from these scant details, we have no surviving record of Fludd's first eighteen years prior to his entrance into St John's College, Oxford in 1592. During 1596 he graduated as Bachelor of Arts, and two years later, at the age of 24, he received his MA.

After obtaining his Master's degree in 1598, Fludd left England for the Continent where he remained for almost six years. Although Thomas Fludd was a man of considerable means, and well able to support his son throughout his travels abroad; Robert chose to supplement his income by tutoring the children of high-born families in Germany, France, Italy and Spain: thus, like Dee, Fludd earned a scholarly reputation.

On his return to England he entered Christ Church Oxford, and there in 1605 he secured a Doctorate in Medicine, but due to his adherence to the 'new' Paracelsian techniques he failed to gain his Fellowship of the Royal College of Physicians. It was not until September 1609 (after three attempts at the examination) that he finally obtained the required qualification and was allowed to practise medicine.

Fludd moved to London where he set up the practice which he was to maintain for the greater part of his life. His curative measures were at that time considered highly unorthodox. Fludd held that the mind and spirit of the patient must be healed first and the disease which afflicted the body second. He engaged a private apothecary who compounded Fludd's 'special medications' on the premises, utilising only the purest materials mixed in exact proportion. Although looked upon disdainfully by his fellow physicians, Fludd's methods of treatment, far removed from the Galenic techniques of his day, were largely successful and highly regarded by an ever growing number of respectful and devoted patients.

Like Forman, Fludd employed astrology as a diagnostic aid; analysed urine samples; and placed much store on the condition of the blood – indeed, one of his close friends was William Harvey the discoverer of the circulatory system. Here the similarity with Forman ends, for Fludd always counselled against the sins of the flesh: advising his patients and associates to avoid drunkenness, gluttony, and womanising (he never married).

Fludd's deep interest in the sciences, music and medicine gradually became more and more integrated with his mystical inclinations. His views on the Kabbalah, magic, divination and alchemy, were often compounded with the laws of harmonics, mechanics and human physiology. These ideas are ensouled in their fullest sense within the pages of his magnum opus: *Utriusque Cosmi . . . Historia* (the History of the Macrocosm and the Microcosm) published during 1617. In this beautifully illustrated work, Fludd gives forth his theories of God, man, and the Universe. The second volume concerns incarnate man, and studies the divinely inspired sciences of astrology, palmistry, prophecy, the art of memory, physiognomy, pyramidology and geomancy.

In the art of geomancy Fludd was an expert, and friends and associates often called upon him to practise his science in answer to matters that troubled them. Geomancy is one of the oldest forms of divination known to man. It involves the construction of sixteen figures derived from the odd or even nature of a series of point marks made in the earth with a wand or stylus, marks on a sheet of paper, or even the random selection of items such as pebbles. Each figure has an attributed Latin name: Puer – boy, Puella – girl, Amissio – loss, Carcer – prison, Via – a way, Populus – people, etc. The figures each composed of four lines of one or two dots, were also held to represent the influences of the planets and zodiacal signs as a further aid to their interpretation. The figure Puer (a boy) ∴ indicated the rash, fiery, impetuous nature of Mars and Aries, the reverse influence of Puella (a girl) ∵ which symbolised the benign powers of Venus and Libra.

While concentrating on the object of the divination the geomantic operator would make sixteen rows of dots in the sand or earth tray, or take sixteen handfuls of pebbles, and then count the number in each row. If the number was even he would make two dots for the first line of the figure, if odd, one dot. This procedure was repeated until the first four figures were generated, by manipulation of these first formed characters (known as the four Mothers) twelve further figures were formed and entered into a chart, or geomantic shield. The derived chart was then analysed with reference to the significance of each figure and the order in which it falls.[1]

Some indication of Fludd's skilled and intuitive application of the art of geomancy can be gleaned from records of his early experiences contained in the second tract of *Historia Macrocosmi* (History of the Macrocosm). Here he states that the hand which makes the geomantic marks 'emanated from the very soul', and errors in the figures were due to 'base and incongruous mutation of the human body'.

In the biographical section of his *History of the Macrocosm* Fludd describes one of his early geomantic exercises in the following words:

> In the penultimate year of the life and reign of the glorious Queen Elizabeth of England (whose fame will never die) I was compelled to spend the whole winter in the city of Avignon, because the winter was very severe, with so much snow covering the mountains of [St] Bernard that the passage into Italy was entirely blocked. With many other young men of gentle birth and of sound education (former pupils of the Jesuits) I received board and lodgings at the house of a certain captain. One evening, while we were drinking at the table, I discussed philosophical subjects with the others and noticed their various opinions on geomantic astrology. Some of them denied its virtue altogether; others, with whom I sided, defended stoutly the validity of that art. I adduced many arguments whereby I proved myself fairly well versed in geomancy.
>
> The meal being over, I had no sooner repaired to my chamber, when one of my companions followed me there and asked me for our love's sake to try my art (which he said, he had seen was considerable) in the resolution of a problem of some importance which, he said, filled his mind with much anxiety. Having made many excuses, I was at last prevailed upon by his entreaties. So instantly I projected a geomantic scheme for the question he had proposed. This question was: whether a girl with whom he had vehemently fallen in love returned his love with equal fervour, and her entire mind and body, and whether she loved him more than anyone else.
>
> Having drawn my [geomantic] scheme, I assured him that I could rather well describe the nature and bodily disposition of his beloved and, having duly described to him the stature and shape of the girl's body, I indicated also a particular and rather noticeable mark or blot thereon, namely a certain kind of wart on her left eye-lid, which he confessed was there. I said also that the girl delighted in vineyards, and this detail, too, was with pleasure confirmed by him. He said that her mother had for that very reason built her house among the vineyards. Finally I gave the following answer to the question he had proposed: that his beloved was inconstant and by no means steady in her love of him, and that she loved somebody else rather more than him.

Whereupon he said that he had always very much suspected that this was the case and that he was [now] seeing it, as it were, with open eyes.

He left my room in haste and then related to his companions with some admiration the verity and virtue of my art. Yet some of them, who knew the girl rather well, denied altogether that she had any such mark on her eye-lid as I had described, until they talked to her the following day and thus became witnesses of the correctness of that detail which I had discovered to them by the art of geomancy and which even they had never previously noticed.[2]

Aside from his involvement in the fields of geomancy, astrology and the Kabbalah, Fludd experimented in other matters, some of which possessed strange and sinister undertones.

Searching for the quintessence of life, Fludd distilled human blood, and on one occasion claimed to have removed a human head, complete with face, eyes, nose and hair, from the vessel, 'upon which it emitted a frightful noise'. Was Fludd attempting to make the alchemical blood-stone from which Paracelsus is said to have extracted the philosophic mercury; a substance used to feed his Homunculus (little man)? The idea of creating life without the aid of woman, the ultimate proof of man's divinity, would have most certainly appealed to Fludd, who in his own words remained throughout his life an 'unstained virgin'.

Paracelsus (1493–1541), the celebrated alchemist, physician and occultist, writes of his manufacture of the Homunculus:

Take a man's semen and place it in a hermetically-sealed retort, bury in horse manure for forty days and magnetise. During this time, it begins to live and move, and at the end of the forty days it resembles human form, but it is transparent and without body.

Feed daily with the 'arcanum' of human blood (the extract of the blood-stone) and maintained at the constant temperature of a mare's womb, for a period of forty weeks (when) it will grow into a human child, as normal as any child born of woman, yet much smaller. It may be raised and educated like any other child, until it grows older and is able to look after itself.

The Scottish doctor William Maxwell hints darkly at Fludd's possession of a human-magnet which had the power to attract the bodily organs; of this Maxwell states: 'the Fluddian magnet is nothing other than dessicated human flesh, which certainly possesses the greatest attractive power: it should be taken, if possible,

HOLY CROSS CHURCH, BEARSTED, KENT   *Photograph R. E. Cousins*

from a body still warm, and from a man who has died a violent death.'[3]

It is perhaps undoubtable that Fludd's deep and far-reaching researches did from time to time lead him to regions that in his day would be considered 'forbidden knowledge'. But in our modern world of the clone and the test-tube baby, Robert Fludd's memory lives on through his contributions to philosophical thought, psychology, and religion, rather than his triflings with homunculi and the human-magnet.

Robert Fludd died on 8 July 1637 at the age of 63. He was buried in Holy Cross Church Bearsted, beneath a stone which he personally prepared before his death. The year following his interment his nephew Thomas erected a monument (which stands to this day) to his memory. The memorial depicts Fludd sitting beneath his family arms with an open book before him. On the pedestal of the monument a Latin inscription reads:

> *Sacred to the memory of Robert Fludd alias De Fluctibus,* [4] *Doctor of both medicines, who, after a peregrination of some years which he had successfully undertaken in foreign parts to cultivate his intellect, was at last restored to his native land and was elected, not undeservedly, to the society of the famous College of Physicians in London. He peacefully exchanged death for life on the eighth day of the seventh month (July) in the year of Our Lord 1637, at the age of 63.*

> *This urn does not smoke with sumptuous perfumes nor does a fine tomb cover your ashes. What is less mortal, yourself, we alone entrust to you – the monuments of your intellect will live here. For whoever writes and dies like you creates an eternal tomb for all posterity.*

> *Thomas Fludd of Gore Courte in Otham in Kent, Knight, erected this monument to the happy memory of his uncle, in the month of August 1638.* [5]

Notes

1   For further information on the subject of geomancy see *Terrestrial Astrology*, Stephen Skinner, Routledge & Kegan Paul, London, 1980.
2   'Robert Fludd's Theory of Geomancy', tr. C. H. Josten, *Journal of the Warburg and Courtauld Institutes*, Vol. 27, pp. 332–3, 1964.
3   *Gabalia*, Will-Erich Peuckert, Berlin 1967.
4   Fludd's alias 'De Fluctibus' literally means: 'of the waves, or Flood'. He always used the phrase in its given Latin form.
5   For Latin text see photograph.

THE ROBERT FLUDD MONUMENT BEARSTED CHURCH
Photograph R. E. Cousins

SACRVM MEMORIÆ

CLARISS DOCTISSQ₂ VIRI ROBERTI FLVDD
ALIAS DE FLVCTIBVS VTRIVSQ₂ MEDICINÆ
DOCTORIS, QVI POST ALIQVOT ANNORVM
PEREGRINATIONEM QVAM AD RECIPIEN=
DVM INGENII CVLTVM IN TRANSMARINAS
REGIONES FÆLICITER SVSCEPERAT PATRIÆ
TANDEM RESTITVTVS, ET IN CELEBERRIMI
COLLEGII MEDICORVM LONDINENSIS
SOCIETATEM NON IMMERITO ELECTVS,
VITAM MORTE PLACIDE COMMVTAVIT
VIII DIE MENSIS VII^BRIS A°D̃.M.D CXXXVII
ÆTATIS SVÆ LXIII.

MAGNIFICIS HÆC NON SVB ODORIBVS VRNA VAPORAT
CRYPTA TEGIT CINERES NEC SPECIOSA TVOS
QVOD MORTALE MINVS, TIBI TE COMMITTIMVS VNVM
INGENII VIVENT HIC MONVMENTA TVI,
NAM TIBI QVI SIMILIS SCRIBIT MORITVRQ₂; SEPVLCHRVM
PRO TOTA ÆTERNVM POSTERITATE FACIT

HOC MONVMENTVM THOMAS FLVDD DE GORE COVRTE
IN OTHAM APVD CANTIANOS ARMIGER IN FÆLICISSIMAM
CHARISSIMI PATRVI SVI MEMORIAM EREXIT DIE
MENSIS AVGVSTI M.D CXXXVIII.

INSCRIPTION ON THE FLUDD MONUMENT   *Photograph R. E. Cousins*

ARTIST'S IMPRESSION OF TWM SION CATI *By Jane O'Reilly*

VI
Thomas Jones of Tregaron
(1530–1609)
In the Shadow of the Hawk
by Patricia Shore Turner

'He was a man of superior information and by the vulgar
in the age he lived regarded as a magician.'

(Lewys Dwnn: *Heraldic Visitations of Wales between 1586 and 1613 . . .*
ed. S. R. Meyrick, page 7, Llandovery, 1846)

In Wales, as in Scotland, Ireland and the Isle of Man, poetry, song and legend are the substance of literature, indicating patterns of custom, social observance and above all, fantasy. Before I enter into a more detailed consideration of the life and times of Thomas Jones, better known as Twm Sion Cati, examples of the mischievous tricks alleged to have been engaged in by this colourful and flamboyant character are thought to be in order.[1]

Things in real life are not quite as legend has them. But then, the Twm Sion Cati legend has acquired a reality of its own.

It is said of Twm he had a sense of humour. Being informed of a famous highwayman in the area he decided to rob him of his horse. Riding a brokendown nag and taking with him a leather bag of shells he went to meet the highwayman who ordered him to stop and deliver. Twm acted suitably reluctant and threw the bag over the hedge. Furious, the highwayman ordered Twm to hold his horse and jumped over the hedge. Promptly Twm changed horses and galloped off.

Another tale tells of a poor man who needed a pitcher (an earthenware jug with two ears and a lip). Twm agreed to help and together they visited a shop. After deriding some of the wares, Twm informed the seller there was a hole in one – which he instantly denied. Twm desired the seller to see for himself by putting his hand in it while indicating to the poor man to creep out with a pitcher. When the seller announced that he could find no hole, Twm mockingly asked him how else he could have put his hand in – and went away laughing.

On another occasion, he observed a woman selling cloth at a fair. Cunningly he tacked one end to his coat, gave a swift turn twisting it round him, and lost himself in the crowd. Shortly afterwards he met the woman grieving over her loss and condoled with her, lamenting that so many rogues frequented fairs, wondering she should be so careless. He told her he always tacked his own cloth to his coat.

The fascination of caves still holds many people. In folklore there are traditions and stories related about these secret places in which heroes sleep in a deathlike state to be awoken in times of danger. Other tales tell of hidden treasure, mythical beasts or fugitives using them as a safe refuge from the law. Situated on the River Tywi (Towey) about twelve miles north of Llandovery is the cave said to have been frequented by Twm Sion Cati during his 'Robin Hood' activities; and possibly used for his more amorous assignations. 'As Sir John Rhys pointed out: ". . . some of these cave stories . . . reveal to us a hero."'*

Why was there such a desperate need for a Welsh Robin Hood or Rob Roy? Although Henry VII had waived many of the penal laws which deprived Welshmen of the benefits of ordinary citizenship giving preferential treatment to their English overlords, the division of Principality and Marches led to a complete lack of uniformity of law. This ambiguity produced much scope for lawlessness.[2]

The merciless regime of Bishop Rowland Lee in the reign of Henry VIII was far from 'affable to any of the Walshrie'.[3] President between 1534 and 1543 of the Council of the Marches of Wales (Cyngor Cymru a'r Goror), he applied a policy of fierce repression, hunting outlaws and wrongdoers, and hanging them in batches as an example to others. Known as the 'hanging judge' he hated the Welsh, boasting of executing between five and six thousand in six years 'and did not disdain to ride after malefactors in person'.[4]

'The hills behind Tregaron, in Cardiganshire, were infested by people who had been declared outlaws for failing to appear at the Great Sessions of the shire. But whether all outlaws were genuine felons is debatable.'[5]

This state of affairs, together with the high number of Englishmen in positions of authority, did not help the situation in Wales. Fortunately, the tidy-minded administrator Thomas Cromwell rose to power; realising that Rowland Lee's negative policy did not work, for feuds between Welsh uchelwyr[6] and English bureaucrats, between Principality and Marches were rapidly becoming endemic.

Were these contributory causes to future legislature changes? Yes, indeed. A similar situation arose in Scotland with the Massacre of Glencoe (13 February 1692)[7] at the time of William of Orange and

*Celtic Folklore, Volume 2, p. 481, Wildwood House, 1980.

TWM SION CATI'S CAVE   *Photograph R. E. Cousins*

much later with the Accession of the Hanoverian Dynasty in England. It was fortunate indeed that Cromwell dealt with the basic problem in Wales at that time with the most comprehensive code for the whole area since Edward I's Statute of Wales, by incorporating the Seven Charters of Henry VII, in which he contented himself with rewarding his most loyal supporters, waiving certain penal laws, and allowing others to drop into disuse.

A more liberal legislation aimed at the administration of Wales (1534) was placed on the Statute Book. An added improvement followed (27 Henry VIII, c.5, 1536), which provided for the appointment of Justices of the Peace in Chester, Flint, Anglesey, Caernarvon, Merioneth, Cardigan, Carmarthen, Pembroke and Glamorgan. Finally, there was passed the 'Act for laws and justice to be administered in Wales in like form as it is in England' (27 Henry VIII, c.26) commonly known as the 'Act of Union'.[8]

The King in Council might legislate but force of law did not always follow. Violence continued; corrupt officials ruled; power-hungry aristocracy and delinquent Churchmen meddled in county and local affairs. The commonalty suffered: 'Lord Chandos was summoned before the Council of Wales for terrifying juries, threatening an under-sheriff with guns, and protecting highway robbers.'[9]

Twm Sion Cati played cat and mouse with authority. Outlawed for sheep-stealing (he had to live), his merry pranks may have outdone Till Eulenspiegel's but hardly those of the Irish bandit Delany and 'Klim', the Russian robber as described in T. J. Llewelyn Pritchard of Swansea's 'first Welsh novel', 'The Adventures and Vagaries of Twm Sion Catti' (1828) Aberystwyth. Various editions, both legal and piratical, followed.

Regardless of chronology the legend grew. W. F. Deacon wrote, Twm John Catty, The Welch Rob Roy.[10] The terminology is Scottish, referring to Twm as a 'chieftain', the 'clans' he roused and harpers playing their 'inspiriting war-songs'. Another version, basically the same, was entitled: The Life, Exploits, and Death of Twm John Catty, The Celebrated Welch Rob Roy and his beautiful bride Elinor, Lady of Llandisent, The Heiress of Ystrad-Ffin.[11]

W. F. Deacon wrote a play on the same theme as his narrative, The Welsh Rob Roy, performed in 1823 at the Coburg Theatre.

The romance of Twm Sion Cati has extended to the present day. The Cardiff-based Theatr Taliesyn's biennial Indo-Celtic, inter-cultural production this year (13–17 April 1988) was the tale of two outlaws: Twm Siôn Catti, the Welsh Robin Hood and Jesel, the seventeenth-century bandit from an area now part of Gujarat. In addition BBC TV produced a serial Hawkmoor* based on Lynn Hughes' novel of the same title; starring the Welsh actor John Ogwen as Cati and Jane Asher as Lady Jeanne of Ystradffin.

Twm gained his Pardon easily once Elizabeth ascended the Throne. The pardon grant under the Great Seal, bearing the date 1 January 1559, 1 Eliz. was countersigned 'Vaughan'.

Thomas Johns alias Cattaye nuper de Tregaron in Comm Cardigan, Geno. alias dict Thomas Johns alias Catty ac(orae) Tregaron in Com. Card. Genereso alias dicit Thome Jones alias Catty. Gent seu quocunque . . . alio nomine vel cognomine neu additone

*Lynn Hughes, Hawkmoor, Christopher Davies/Penguin, 1977.

hominis cognitonis dignitatus officii seu loci idem Thomas cogna-
tur vocetur seu nuneupatur . . . Omnia escapia et cautiones.[12]

Unfortunately the transcription of the Pardon has not been given in
full in *The History of Tregaron* and certain copying errors are apparent in
the printed version. However, these may have been due to the state of
the original manuscript or the difficulty in reading the Elizabethan hand.

Cf. Christopher Upton's corrected version with the differences in
italics:

> Thomas Johns alias Cattaye nuper de Tregaron in *Comm.*
> Cardigan, Gen*eroso* alias *dicitur* Thomas Johns alias Catty ac
> (orae) Tregaron in Com. Card. Generoso alias *dicitur* Thomas
> Jones alias Catty *Gent.* seu quocunque . . . alio nomine vel
> cognomine neu *additione* hominis *cognationis* dignitatus officii seu
> loci idem Thomas cognatur vocetur seu nuncupatur . . . omnia
> escapia et cautiones. [Thomas Johns alias Cattaye late of Tre-
> garon in the county of Cardigan, gent., otherwise called
> Thomas Johns alias Catty and of the region of Tregaron in the
> county of Cardigan, gent; otherwise called Thomas Jones alias
> Catty, gent; whether by any other name or cognomen or by a
> man's title, device, office, position or place the same Thomas be
> known, called or named . . . all fines (for escape) and debts.]

Born Thomas Jones of Fountain Gate (Porth-y-ffynon) Tregaron;
Twm was the natural son[13] of John, son of David ap Madog ap Howel
Moethau ap Rees Moethau (the latter was living in 1399, and was
fourth in descent from Griffith Voel, descended from Gwaethfod
Fawr, Prince of Ceredigion), and by Catherine, natural daughter of
Meredydd ap Ieuan ap Robert.[14] In 1588 Twm is described as a man
of good family, his armorial bearings being those of Gwaethfod.

The gentry of Wales were principally a squirearchy living semi-
rural lives; in many cases their limited means led their existence to
seem barely distinguishable from that of the richer yeomen. However, skilful manipulation of the English land laws, matrimonial
arrangements, selective property purchases and other, not so legal,
methods gained substantial estates for some. But most of the Welsh
gentry remained relatively poor, their land realising incomes of less
than £100 per year.

Thomas Jones claimed kinship with the powerful Cecil (Seisyllt)
family, advisors to the English throne, and inter-marital connections
with the Herberts, the Vaughans of Tyle-glas, and the Clements,
lords of Caron, among others. According to the Lay Subsidies and
Plea Rolls, (*Trans. Carm. Ant. Soc. Vol. 9. p. 16*) Thomas Jones'
uncle, Rees ap David ap Madoc (1560), and his cousin, Evan ap

Rosser ap David (1576), were at Caron at those dates. As Owen notes: 'To the Welsh gentleman, his pedigree was a matter of deep concern. For one thing, it established his kinship and relations with other families pertaining to the squirearchy'.[15] Thus gentlemen of a literary or antiquarian inclination, like Thomas Jones, engaged in the study of genealogy as a serious pursuit.

After Henry VII cautiously extended English common law into Wales and the Act of Union (1535) was passed by Henry VIII, Wales was compelled to accept English laws. For the gentry, this meant, above all, that land left by a deceased father now passed to the eldest son rather than being divided equally between all the sons: in effect, the rule of primogeniture over gavelkind.

Numerous manuscripts of the period show how deeply attached the squires were to details of their genealogy, for it justified their claim to social pretensions, family pride and self-esteem, since it showed that their ancestors had been the natural leaders of the Welsh people.

Twm was a singer and poet. According to R. Isgarn Davies, Twm won the Chair at Llandaff Eisteddfod in 1561.

Twm's poetry is widely scattered. For example, 'Cywydd y Gofid', an 'Ode to Grief', or 'Poem of Affliction', is included in S. R. Meyrick's *History of Cardiganshire*, p. 249; it is printed also in *Yr Haul* (December 1845). Other poems may be found in *British Museum, Additional MSS. 14907, 15008, 15056.*

Apparently Twm collected many of the Triads, as the following note, in translation, from the London edition of a transcription shows: 'The Triads were taken from the book of Caradoc of Nant-carven, and from the book of Jevan Brechva, by me Thomas Jones, of Tregaron; and these are all I could get of the three hundred, 1601'.[16]

The following eulogium by his contemporary Dr John David Rhys cannot but show the respect Twm had gained:

> Whoever professes himself to be a Herald Bard, must know the pedigrees of Kings and Princes, and be skilled in the works of the three chief Bards of the Isles of Britain: namely Merlin, son of Morvyn, Merlin Ambrosius, and Taliesin the Chief Bard. ('Myrdhin ab Morbrynn, a Myrdhin Emrys, a Thaliessin Benn Beirdh'). And in the Science of Heraldry, with respect to being thoroughly acquainted with the real descents, armorial bearings, dignities, and illustrious actions of the nobility and gentry of Wales, the most celebrated accomplished and accurate (and that beyond doubt) is reckoned Tomas Sion, alias Moethau, of Porth-y-ffynnon, near Trev Garon (Thomas Jones of Fountayn

Gate). And when he is gone, it will be a very doubtful chance
that he will be able for a long time to leave behind him an equal,
nor indeed any genealogist (with regard to being so conversant
as he in that science) that can ever come near him.[17]

Various pedigrees are said to be the work of Thomas Jones. J. Kyle
Fletcher, for example, in his article, *City's Treasury of Old Welsh
Books*[18] comments on the Family Rolls (pedigree rolls) thus:

> . . . but the finest one is the roll of the Kendrick family in rich
> colours, tricked with gold and silver. Written during the reign
> of Elizabeth this roll is the work of that well-known Herald
> Bard, Thomas Jones, of Fountain Gate, usually called "Twm
> Shon Catti".

Mr R. Isgarn Davies gives the following:

> His pedigree of Charles Morgan, in the British Museum (z.20,
> 1066, Harleian Roll) is in beautiful handwork and colouring, the
> wording being as follows:
> 'Pedigree of Charles Morgan of Arheston, Esq., Usher in
> Ordinary to Queen Elizabeth . . . by Thomas Jones of Tre-
> garon, 1577. This Genealogie . . . is here set downe accordinge
> unto divers Recordes and manye verye good presidents collect-
> ed by Thomas Joanes of Tregaron in Wales, gentilman, in the
> yeare of our Lord 1577. Exemplified and Augmented by Philip
> Holand, Role persevant of Armes, 1602.'
> Also – (F.117.B. Brit. Museum MSS): 'Herbert, earl of
> Pembroke, as it was set forth by Thomas Jones of Tregaron, AD
> 1582'.
> Also – (F.52. Brit. Museum MSS, 506, 2012): 'Sir Thomas
> Moston of Moston, set forth by Thomas Jones of Tregaron, and
> fynished at Founteyne Gate the 9th March, 1604'.[19]

Again Meyrick states: 'At Nant-Eôs is an emblazoned pedigree of
the Corbet family written and painted by him'.
Well had Thomas Jones earned the honoured title of 'Herald Bard'.
Unexpectedly, another personality of the age was soon to enter the
Welsh scene, a personality who became also both famous and
infamous in his own lifetime: '1579. Nov. 29th. *I receyved a letter from
Mr Thomas Jones*', wrote Dr John Dee in his *Private Diary*.[20]
John Dee, a member of the extensive Welsh circle in London, was
the son of Rowland Dee, Gentleman Server to Henry VIII; in effect,
he was chief carver at the King's Table and managed the royal
kitchen. Unfortunately for Rowland Dee he was a rather rash Welsh
patriot who boasted injudiciously of the royal blood in his veins; thus

he came to be regarded as an arrogant upstart by his royal master who treated him in contemptible fashion refusing him preferment.

John Dee, however, took great pride in his Welsh ancestry ('Dee' is the anglicised version of *Dhu*, meaning black), an ancestry dating back to Rhodri the Great, King of Wales. Also his great-grandfather Dafydd Dhu (Will dated 1412) was descended from Llewelyn Crugeryr, a chieftain, and another ancestor was Rhys ap Tewdr, prince of South Wales in 1077. To this extent the Dee family had a distant connection with the Royal House of Tudor.[21]

Twm and John Dee shared a keen interest in genealogy, antiquarianism, poetry and many other subjects.

Dee's home in Mortlake appears to have been a somewhat rambling property to which he added rooms and buildings from time to time. This building housed five rooms of books and his many collections. In connection with his British Isles antiquarian studies he gathered Welsh and Irish records, genealogies and ancient seals,[22] ever seeking to encourage a wider interest in the British language, culture and its ancient legends. Also, he sought to discover the whereabouts of manuscripts about the Welsh Bards.

Dee's continued interest revealed itself in 1574. He writes of 'Certaine verie rare observations of Chester: and some parts of Wales: with divers Epitaphes Coatarmours and other monuments verie orderlie and labouriouslie gathered together'. Briefly, this is the record of a short antiquarian tour. Dee began at Chester, travelling from Westchester via Pulford to Gresford (23 August). He stayed at Wrexham on 24 August (St Bartholomew's Day). Later, he went to Bangor and Oswestry, and spent 30 August at Presteigne. He met Mr Pryce the Mayor at Hereford on Wednesday, 1 September. Also, he recorded going to Ledbury via the Malvern Hills and visited a Mr Edward Threlkeld, Chancellor of Hereford, 'one of my old acqyantance syns K. Edward his tyme'. From there he travelled to Gloucester then Cirencester.[23]

Dee maintained his links with Wales throughout his life and, it appears, especially with Thomas Jones. He wrote, '1590. Nov. 28th . . . My cousin Mr Thomas Junes cam in the ende of the terme about St Andrew's even.' And again in the same year: 'Dec. 6th. Mr Thomas Griffith my cosen from Llanbeder cam to see me, and lay all night with me, and allso Mr Thomas Jones, and in the Monday morning went by water to London, and so the same day homeward. A meridie circa 3ᵃ recipi a Regina Domina £50.'

One could speculate as to whether the payment from the Queen's Majesty was for information brought by Twm.

On 8 January 1595 the Wardenship of Christ's College, Manchester, was offered to Dee through the influence of Archbishop Whitgift. When this was confirmed by Elizabeth, Dee accepted the post. However, he did not forget his Welsh connection. As he wrote in his *Private Diary*: '1596. July 9th. I sent Roger Kay of Manchester with my letters into Wales.' And, 'Aug. 10th. Mr Thomas Jones of Tregaron cam to me to Manchester and rode towards Wales bak again the 13th day to mete the catall coming. Aug. 13th. I rid toward York. Halifax and Mr Thomas Jones rode toward Wales.' By 'Sept. 5th. seventeen hed of cattell from my kinsfolk in Wales by the curteous Griffith David nephew to Mr Thomas Griffith, brought'.

One might consider whether the 'Griffith David' mentioned by Dee is the same man Twm's daughter Margaret married? In Twm's Will[24] one of the debts mentioned was one from Griffith David, 'my son-in-law'.

The gentry rarely went outside their own social circle when they arranged marriages. Primarily, what interested them was the territorial or financial benefits accruing from an advantageous alliance within their own class, since they had little to gain from marriages with their inferiors. Thus they evolved a system of marriage alliances that closely knit the landed families of North and South Wales. This extended the influence and consolidated the power of the Welsh gentry into what could, and indeed did later, become a potent political and military force.

Power and influence could be misused. On a certain Sunday in 1599 Richard Price, head of the Gogerddan family, 'requested' the men of Cardiganshire to meet him at the parish church of Tregaron. The countryfolk were met by five hundred armed retainers who forced them into the church to hear divine service. After this enforced act of piety they found a platter set out on the churchyard stile. Richard Price announced a *comortha* (voluntary payment) for which he, and four other Justices of the Peace, would be duly grateful. 'He added, however, that anyone failing to show an exemplary liberality would run the risk of being pressed for military service in Ireland.'[25] An effective speech that produced £100.

Greedily, Price arranged for his wife to initiate *comorthas* amongst the women of north Cardiganshire enabling him to add £200 to his personal fortune. Other Justices of the Peace followed this example taking even lambs and calves in their own *comorthas* and giving thanks for them.

Violence abounded even amongst the clergy. We read for example of '. . . Ieuan Gwyn, a priest . . . drawing his rapier and dagger upon another member of the clerical fraternity in the chancel of Clyro Church, in Radnorshire, and wounding him in the head'.[26]

Many of the clergy were also corrupt, leading lives that were no good example to their unfortunate parishioners: 'The preponderantly secular outlook of the Church, its largely effete clergy and the many abuses that they committed, were bound to contribute towards . . . spiritual malaise.'[27]

The actions of one Morgan Davyd, clerk, vicar of Caron verged on paranoia. Thomas Jones issued a Bill of Complaint[28] to the Court of Star Chamber on 3 November 1601, listing an amazing total of events concerning Morgan Davyd.

Thomas Jones accused the Vicar of 'greater wealth than learning' and of 'continual stirring up of strife'. Also, that he went round armed and assaulted his parishioners when the fancy took him. But the main tale is of the constant feud waged against Thomas Jones himself.

Morgan Davyd, with the aid of his servants and one Gwenllian verch David, let horses and cattle into fields sown with corn, wheat and barley causing £40 worth of damage to Twm's crops. When John Moythe objected, the Vicar beat him so severely he lost the use of one arm. Eleanor Pryce ran out of Fountain Gate to aid John Moythe and was attacked in her turn and dragged from the courtyard by her hair.

Not content with these deliberate outrages against Twm's servants, when drunk (as he frequently was) the Vicar and up to ten of his people attacked one Jenckyn Tyler who was repairing the Church roof. Blaspheming God and swearing against Thomas Jones he broke up two ladders 'armed with a great axe' and 'his sword by his side', and threatened Jenckyn Tyler or any of his friends that 'he would cut them in as many pieces as one of the ladders'.

The Vicar had not finished with Twm's retainers. On 9 July 1598 he and his servants plotted to murder John Moythe. Arming themselves, they caught the unfortunate young man going up the hillside and, after beating him, dragged him to a tree and attempted to hang him. Moythe made so much noise the neighbours rescued him and bore him, half-dead, home to Fountain Gate.

Morgan Davyd continually attacked Fountain Gate and its servants. He played various tricks and even Twm himself was injured several times.

Rees ap Ieuan Gitto sent his wife and two retainers to serve 'your Majesty's process out of your Court of Exchequer' and the 'said Morgan Davyd, most contemptiously and irreverently took the said process and threw it to the ground and trod it under his feet in the dirt'.

Murder still on his mind, Morgan Davyd resolved to stab Twm as he sat in the Leet Court as Steward of the lordship of Caron (16 April 1601). The bloodthirsty Vicar concealed a dagger inside his shirt and crept towards Thomas Jones. But he was noticed and apprehended, whereon he swore to kill Twm by any means, notwithstanding what death he had to suffer afterward. The claspknife in Carmarthen

CLASPKNIFE Inscribed 'T. Jones, Tregaron' with 1606 on reverse.
Courtesy Carmarthen Museum

Museum may have been Twm's souvenir of the incident. (See photograph.)

Twm Sion Cati defended his retainers, property and the local folk against the evil Churchman. The Pardoned Welsh Robin Hood still sallied forth, previously into, but now against, lawlessness. Throughout his life Twm had lived dangerously, and his new respectability did not alter this.

Twm's home may well have been a fortified farmhouse, a safe retreat from the Vicar's men when the gates were shut. Apart from the fields of crops he kept cattle. The need for fortification is apparent when noting the long list of weapons the Vicar and his followers brought out against Twm, his retainers and the village folk: sword and dagger, a long bastynado or cudgel, a long pike of iron, a great axe, a main pike, a gleve,[29] a giant gleve, pitchforks and different kinds of javelins.

Twm married twice, fathering three children, Rhys, Margaret and an illegitimate son, John Moythe. In his Will, dated 17 May 1609, he made a bequest of 'to John Moythe, my base son, 9 cattle', who in the Bill of Complaint is referred to as 'a menial servant of your subject'.

Eleanor Pryce, another relative, was said to be 'your subject's maid servant' and 'your subject's cousin'.

His second marriage to Joan Williams of Ystradffin, Rhandiemwyn, widow of Thomas Rhys Williams, a wealthy landowner and daughter of Sir John Price of the Priory of Brecon, adds greatly to legend.

Fact and fiction meet in curious fashion. A strange sequence of events began to take place at Ystradffin. Joan's aged husband made his Will early September 1607 and died shortly afterwards. Joan married Thomas Jones within that same month.

So that Joan could retain £200 worth of gold and silver jewellery in addition to over £3,000 in land and goods legally left her, Thomas Jones and her brother-in-law John Winter helped her to alter her late husband's Will. However, the Executors, Thomas Phillipes, Gregorie Morris and William Lloyd, complained before the Star Chamber that, 'Thomas Jones et Joan uxor, late wife of the said Thomas Williams' had falsified her late husband's Will and had detained his goods.[30]

In an undated petition to Robert Cecil, Lord Salisbury, Twm requested that 'an action againgst him may be transferred to the local court on account of his old age'; and adds further that Lord Burghley 'did recon me to be his kinsmane, for that he was descended from my greate graunfather, Howell Moythey'.[31]

But the 'heiress of Ystradffin' had yet another suitor, Sir George Devereux, tenant of Llwynybrain near Llandovery. (He had been deeply involved in the rebellion against Elizabeth and was uncle to the Earl of Essex,[32] who on 25 February 1601, Ash Wednesday, at 8.00 a.m. was beheaded with one stroke of the axe. (See: CSP Domestic, 1598–1601, 588.))

J. Frederick Jones, in *Thomas Jones of Tregaron alias Twm Shon Catti (1530–1609)*, states, 'On the floor of one of the bedrooms at Ystradffin there is a strange indestructible red patch which is supposed to be a bloodstain'. He speculated on the 'origin of the stain which I saw as recently as the summer in 1935'.

'Did Sir George Devereux, aided by Joan stealthily murder poor Thomas Jones at dead of night?' And yet again, 'Did Thomas Jones obligingly die of old age after making his Will in Joan's favour, or is that everlasting stain the only evidence of his sudden departure at the dagger's point?'

Alas, on this point history is silent. Naturally, Joan married Sir George Devereux for women were 'hardened by the repetition of the marriage vow'.[33]

Twm died in affluent, if mysterious, circumstances. In contrast Dr John Dee, his cousin and correspondent for so many years died in extreme poverty at his home in Mortlake, tended only by his loyal daughter Katherine and ministered to by his son Arthur. His beloved, faithful wife Jane Fromond had died of the plague in 1605, leaving the old scholar lonely in his last years.

Nowadays nothing can be seen of Fountain Gate (Porth-y-ffynon) except a grass covered site.

'His home was a charming old house built out of the ruins of an old HAFOD which had belonged to the Gwaethfod family.'[34]

In 1894, when stones from the ruined walls were removed, two sandstone blocks, each bearing a heraldic emblem, were discovered and carefully preserved by Mr H. O. Evans of Werna. Hence these two blocks came to be known as '*The Werna Stones*'. (See photograph.) These two stones are cherished and likewise preserved today in Tregaron Secondary School Museum.

The *Western Mail*, 2 March 1926 stated thus:

> on two of the stones it will be seen that the coat of arms is that of the TEWDWR family. One was engrail and the other bordered (plain).
>
> Dr Cyril Fox said that the dating of the heraldic carved stones which presented a lion rampart, one within an engrailed, the other within a plain border and with initials under . . . The letters showed notched serifs, and had bosses or expansions on the central line, e.g. of the 'I' and the curve of the 'D'. These features are normally found in inscriptions of the first half of the sixteenth century . . . I suggest they probably come from a house erected immediately after the Dissolution – about 1550 – a time, when, all over the country squires, enriched by monastic estates, were building new large houses. (*Arch. Camb. LXXXVI. Part 2, p. 386.*)

Such heraldic stones would have been regarded as precious, 'Tewdwr' being a princely family, and would have been carefully built into one of the inner walls of Porth-y-ffynon.

A third stone with different carving and without initials was taken from the ruins, in about 1868, and built into the wall of the home of the late Mr John Philip Rees, a mason descended from a long line of masons and Parish Clerk (1865–1904). However, despite an intensive search for this stone undertaken in Doldre by Robin E. Cousins and friends no trace of this third stone can be found. The suggestion has been put forward that modern progress probably cemented it over.

In *Tregaron, The W.I. looks around its Town and Country* a fourth stone is mentioned on page 31. Earlier in this excellent booklet, on page 27, it notes:

THE WERNA STONES   *Courtesy Tregaron Secondary School*

towards Port Einon, you pass Neuadd Las, a modern bungalow standing on the very ancient industrial site of a flint chipping floor in Mesolithic times, probably when Gors Caron was a lake . . . On the other bank of the river (Afon Teifi) lies Penybont Farm, whose farmhouse, once a modest country mansion, was built in 1630 by the grandfather of the renowned Thomas Johnes of Hafod.

The Celtic lands abound in folktales of underwater cities and palaces – Sir John Rhys recorded that in the late nineteenth century Welsh mothers still warned their children not to stray too far from their homes when the mist was thick lest they should be snatched away by the fairies to their dwellings beneath the lakes.

Tregaron has a fascinating legend that sounds very much like a Welsh version of Sodom and Gomorrah. North of Tregaron is Llyn-y-Maes, a small lake. Old Tregaronians (it is said) indulged themselves nightly in exotic revelry, great feasts and lewd orgies. Naturally, the long-bearded prophet warned them of fire, flood and destruction if they did not mend their ways – alas, to no avail . . . One night lightning struck, setting the village afire, following which came a flood overwhelming every one of the revellers; those not burnt were drowned and the village sank slowly into the waters of the lake. It sounds like the kind of tale Vicar Morgan Davyd would have preached to his parishioners. The legend may have originated from the logs in the peat from the adjacent bog which is the largest

SWALLOW-TAILED KITE *by Jane O'Reilly*

outside Ireland in the British Isles. 'Now it is the haunt of students of botany, zoology and geomorphology, and increasingly of bird-watchers eager to see the Red Kite in its main breeding ground'.[35]

So to a conclusion: having set Thomas Jones in his rightful historical context, what of his role as Twm Sion Cati, the Welsh Robin Hood? It must be remembered that the dominant philosophy of the Tudor Era was not only that of serious theologians, hard-headed politicians and ambitious seamen but a world where spirits, fairies, and conjurors found their way into the poetry of the age. The preoccupation of both high and low rank found expression in the enchantment of myth and legend, popular traditions and the extension of magic penetrating into profound spheres of all knowledge and experience.

I like to think of Twm, his dark handsome face appearing out of the gloom playing tricks on corrupt authority or fishing salmon from the Teifi, meditating on a poem to his latest love. May he live long in the folklore of Wales.

Notes

1 These tales are to be found in S. R. Meyrick, *History of Cardiganshire*, 1810, pp. 247–51.
2 Glyn Roberts, *Aspects of Welsh History*, p. 25.

3   A. H. Dodd, *Life In Wales*, Chapter IV, p. 63.

4   Ibid.

5   G. Dyfnallt Owen, *Elizabethan Wales*, p. 172.

6   'uchelwyr' (plural), gentlemen, noblemen, superiors. *The New Collins Spurrell Welsh Dictionary*, 1960.

7   Derick S. Thomson (ed.) *The Companion to Gaelic Scotland*, Basil Blackwell, 1983.

8   For detail see Glyn Roberts, *Aspects of Welsh History*, Political Affairs from 1536 to 1900, p. 27.

9   Paul Johnson, *Elizabeth I*, Omega, Futura Publications, 1976.

10   The Innkeeper's Album, London, 1823.

11   Published by J. L. Marks, 17 Artillery-street, Bishopsgate, London, Six-pence, 1830.

12   D. C. Rees, *The History of Tregaron*, 1936, p. 105.

13   'Bastard sons and daughters suffered no harm from the conditions of their birth. They were not socially ostracised nor discriminated against by their reputed fathers. On the contrary, they were publicly recognised, enjoyed the protection of the families into which they had been adventitiously born, and were bequeathed property and gifts like the more legitimate offspring. And no one, not even the Church, showed much disapproval of this behaviour.' (G. Dyfnallt Owen, *Elizabethan Wales*, p. 17)

14   Detail from pedigree dated 30 December 1588 supplied by Thomas Jones to Lewys Dwnn.

15   G. Dyfnallt Owen, *Elizabethan Wales*, p. 13.

16   'A'r Trioedd hynn a dynnwyd o Lyfyr Caradawc Nant Garfyn, ac o Lyfyr Ieuan Brechfa, gannof fi Thomas Jones o Dregaron; a hynn e ellais i gael o'r trichant – 1601'. (*The Myfyrian Archaiology*, 1870, p. 411).

17   Dr J. D. Rhys, *Linguae Cymraecae Institutiones Accuratae* (1592), p. 303. Translated from the Welsh by S. R. Meyrick.

18   *Western Mail*. Wednesday, 17 August 1938, p. 6.

19   R. Isgarn Davies, *Thomas Jones (Twm Shon Catti), Porth-y-ffynon, Bard, Genealogist, Antiquary and Gentleman*. (From, D. C. Rees, *The History of Tregaron*, 1936.)

20   *The Private Diary of Dr John Dee* (ed. James O. Halliwell, Camden Society, London, 1842).

21   See the Genealogical Rolls in the British Museum: Cotton Charter XIII, art.38. Pedigree by John Dee tracing his ancestry to the earliest Welsh princes. Cotton Charter XIV, art.1. traces the ancestry of Elizabeth and John Dee back to the earliest Welsh Kings. Harleian MS. 5835, art.2. Dee's own pedigree. Oxford. See Ashmole MS.847. fols. 1^v·, 118^v· Marginal notes made by Dee concerning some of his Welsh relatives.

22   John Dee, *Compendious Rehearsal*, pp. 27–31.

23   British Museum, Harleian MS. 473.

24   Will of Thomas Jones, Caron, alias Twm Sion Catti, AD 1609. In the Carmarthen Registry. (Transactions of the Carmarthen Antiquarian Soc. and Field Club, Vol. 9, p. 16, 1913.)

25   G. Dyfnallt Owen, *Elizabethan Wales*, p. 27.

26   *Ibid.*, pp. 227–8.

27   *Ibid.*, pp. 227–8.

28   *Welsh Gazette*, Thursday, 24 May and Thursday, 31 May 1928.

29   Gleve or glaive: 'From the 13th to 15th centuries English writers used this word as an equivalent of lance; from then on, it has been used to indicate a sword or a dagger. When used by modern writers on arms, the word usually indicates a staff weapon with a knifelike blade'. (William Reid, *Arms Through The Ages*, p. 273. A. B. Nordbok, Gothenburg, Sweden, 1976.)

30   Star Chamber Proceedings, James I, 241/11.

31   Calendar of State Papers, Domestic Series, James I, 1611–18, Vol. LXIX, p. 130. Letters and Papers, numbers 11–15 (undated).

32   Strangely enough the first few passages from Dr John Dee's *Liber Logaeth* (*The Book of the Speech of God* or *The Sixth Book of the Holy Mysteries – Liber Mysteriorum Sixtus et Sanctus*) together with a small amount of material based on Dee's Angelic experiments can be found bound up together with a manuscript peculiarly entitled, *The Self-murder of the Earl of Essex* in B. M. Sloane MS. 78. art. 11.

33   G. Dyfnallt Owen, *Elizabethan Wales*, p. 16.

34   J. Kyle Fletcher, *Western Mail*, 22 August 1921. '*hafod*' – summer dwelling (*Gwasg-gomer Dictionary*).

35   Tregaron W. I., *Tregaron, the W.I. looks around its Town & Country*, p. 26.

ROBERT TURNER Portrait from Turner's *Compleat Bone-setter*.
Courtesy British Library Board

VII
Robert Turner of 'Holshott'
(C. 1620 – 1665?)
The Astrological Botanist and the Books of the Elizabethan Magi
by Robin E. Cousins

Robert Turner lived during the seventeenth century and is known today for his translations of important magical and alchemical texts, mostly dating from the fifteenth and sixteenth centuries. These works include such famous titles as the *Ars Notoria: the Notary Art of Solomon, Of the Supreme Mysteries of Nature* by Paracelsus, and Henry Cornelius Agrippa's *Fourth Book of Occult Philosophy*. Such treatises were highly influential in Elizabethan occult circles, even though they were written in Latin and sometimes only available in manuscript form. John Dee, for example, was strongly influenced by Agrippa, whose works he often consulted during the course of magical experiments. Dee possessed an awesome library of nearly 4,000 printed books and manuscripts, which included large sections devoted to the works of Paracelsus (1493–1541) and Ramon Lull (1234–1316). The library was at the disposal of Dee's circle of friends and was even visited by Queen Elizabeth on 10 March 1575. Occult writings, such as Dee possessed, were virtually inaccessible to the general public and could be so today, if it were not for the scholastic labours of Robert Turner. His work has helped to provide an insight into the magical world of the sixteenth century, not only for his contemporaries, but for occultists and researchers ever since.

Although Turner flourished fifty years after John Dee, who had died in 1608, his translations helped to keep the Elizabethan hermetic tradition alive, long after the glory of that era had faded. The translations have never been surpassed and are frequently consulted by the twentieth-century magician. Turner's translation of the *Fourth Book* has been particularly influential. The book is attributed to Agrippa (1486–1535) and was originally published in Latin at Marburg in 1559. Dee owned a copy of this edition; but, as a result of

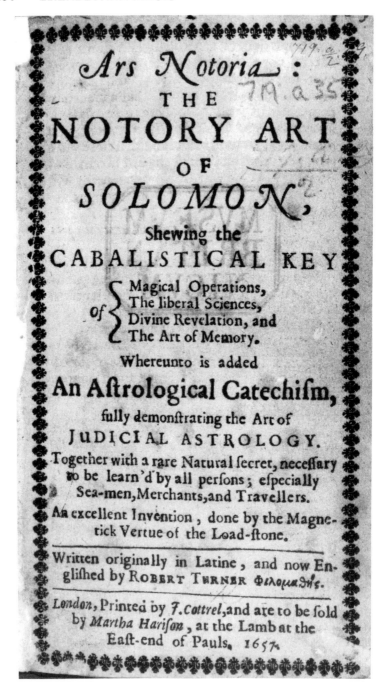

Ars Notoria :

THE

NOTORY ART

OF

SOLOMON,

Shewing the

CABALISTICAL KEY

of { Magical Operations,
The liberal Sciences,
Divine Revelation, and
The Art of Memory.

Whereunto is added

An Astrological Catechism,

fully demonstrating the Art of

JUDICIAL ASTROLOGY.

Together with a rare Natural secret, necessary
to be learn'd by all persons; especially
Sea-men, Merchants, and Travellers.

An excellent Invention, done by the Magne-
tick Vertue of the Load-stone.

Written originally in Latine, and now Englished by ROBERT TURNER Φιλομαθής.

London, Printed by *J. Cottrel*, and are to be sold
by *Martha Harison*, at the Lamb at the
East-end of Pauls, 1657.

TITLE-PAGE OF ARS NOTORIA – Translated by Robert Turner, 1657
Courtesy British Library Board

Turner's translation, by the 1670s no self-respecting astrologer or herbalist could be found without a copy of the book upon their table. Over a hundred years later, Francis Barrett employed the translation when compiling *The Magus* (1801). He notes that the *Fourth Book* was 'unavailable except for large amounts', thereby demonstrating the worth of Turner's work. This was echoed by A. E. Waite, a man seldom free with compliments, who decided to 'depart from my usual custom of translating at first hand and make use . . . of the version of Robert Turner, which is quite faithful and has, moreover, the pleasant flavour of antiquity'.[1]

The *Fourth Book* also incorporates Turner's translations of five additional magical manuscripts, including *Of Geomancy* which is attributed to Agrippa; the *Heptameron; or Magical Elements* which is ascribed to Peter de Abano (1250–1317) and gives specific details on the invocation of angels; the *Isagoge* by Georg Pictorius von Villingen (*c.*1500–1569) which was published in Basel in 1563; *Astronomical Geomancy* possibly by Gerard of Cremona (1114–1187); and the *Arbatel of Magick*, an anonymous work published in Basel in 1575. Dee certainly possessed works by Peter de Abano, who had been accused of practising sorcery. After his death, Peter was burnt in effigy and the reading of his 'abominable' books was forbidden.

Both the *Fourth Book* and *Of the Supreme Mysteries of Nature* are still in demand and were republished recently, the latter book being entitled *Archidoxes of Magic* (1975). The *Ars Notoria* was reprinted in 1987, but unfortunately omits Turner's introduction.

In his day Robert Turner was equally well-known as an able astrologer and herbalist, and his later books reflect this interest. In 1664 Turner published his herbal, ΒΟΤΑΝΟΛΟΓΙΑ. *The Brittish Physician* [Botanologia], which was based on the Doctrine of Signatures and was similar to Culpeper's herbal of 1653. Turner also wrote and translated medical works and compounded herbal medicines for the plague and other ailments. He sold the medicines direct to the public from his house in Christopher Alley,[2] near St Paul's, and through his booksellers. He claimed his remedies far exceeded the 'intellect of the Modern Speculator of Spittlefields', thereby revealing his dislike of the successful Nicholas Culpeper.

The Early Years

Biographical details of Robert Turner are sketchy. The entry in the *Dictionary of National Biography* (DNB) is short and is mostly devoted to a description of his publications. His books, however, do provide some knowledge of his ideas and the occasional biographical detail. Other sources of information are scarce and, unfortunately, the local

THE BRITTISH or ENGLISH PHYSITIAN.

ΒΟΤΑΝΟΛΟΓΙΑ.

THE

Brittish Physician :

OR,

The NATURE and VERTUES

OF

ENGLISH PLANTS.

Exactly defcribing fuch Plants as grow Naturally in our Land, with their feveral Names, Greek, Latine, or Englifh, Natures, Places where they grow, Times when they flourifh, and are moft proper to be gathered; their degrees of Temperature, Applications and Vertues, Phyfical and Aftrological Ufes, treated of; each Plant appropriated to the feveral Difeafes they cure, and directions for their Medicinal Ufes, throughout the whole Body of Man; being moft fpecial helps for fudden Accidents, Acute and Chronick Diftempers.

By means whereof People may gather their own Phyfick under every Hedge, or in their own Gardens, which may be moft conducing to their Health; fo that obferving the direction in this Book, they may become their own Phyficians: For what Climate foever is fubject to any particular Difeafe, in the fame place there grows a Cure.

With two exact Tables; the one of the Englifh and Latine Names of the Plants; the other of the Difeafes and Names of each Plant appropriated to the Difeafes, with their Cures.

By *Robert Turner*, Botanolog. Stud.

London, Printed for *Obadiah Blagrave*, at the *Black Bear* and *Star* in St. *Pauls Church-Yard*, over againft the Little North-Door, 1 6 8 7.

TITLE-PAGE OF ROBERT TURNER'S ΒΟΤΑΝΟΛΟΓΙΑ. 1687
Courtesy British Library Board

parish records of Christchurch, Newgate Street, for the period from 1588 to September 1666 were destroyed in the Great Fire. In fact, until now the DNB provided the most extensive information available. It is from this work that the description 'Robert Turner of Holshott' is derived, which effectively distinguishes him from other famous namesakes. The former manor of Holdshott was the home of Turner's father for some years and is today part of the parish of Heckfield in North Hampshire. His father lived in the extreme south of the parish by some boggy ground, adjoining the Grove Copse. Turner describes himself as 'Robert Turner of Holshott' in four of his books and dedicates the works to notables of neighbouring villages, even though the books themselves bear a London address.

Little is known of Turner's early life. He was born in 'my Countrey of Hampshire'[3] about 1620, but not necessarily in Holdshott. The local parish registers do not contain any reference to him, although Turners certainly lived in the area at the time. On 17 June 1636, at the age of 16, he was admitted to Christ's College, Cambridge, from where he matriculated as a Pensioner. Most undergraduates belonged to this class and were mainly the sons of small landowners, the clergy, or the fairly 'well-to-do'. Poorer students were known as 'Sizars', while the sons of the landed gentry or the aristocracy were called 'Fellow Commoners'. Sizars were invariably servants to their tutors or the Fellows, in order to help with expenses – a problem which did not affect Robert Turner, whose tutor was a certain Mr Brearley. On 9 October 1637, Turner was admitted at the Middle Temple. He obtained his BA in 1639 and entered Lincoln's Inn during the November of that year.

The Inns of Court were considered as finishing schools for wealthy young men from Oxford or Cambridge. They continued their education with the study of law at one of the Inns and about 80 per cent of the intake came from the landed classes. Even if they did not intend to practise, a knowledge of the law was always useful to gentlemen of property, especially during the later seventeenth century, when dealing with the many disputes resulting from the land confiscations of The Commonwealth. Unlike many, however, Turner did choose to practise the law, although apparently not until the late 1650s. On 14 June 1665, he is described as a 'frequent solicitor',[4] and, indeed, his name is recorded in the *Calendar of State Papers* on several occasions between 1658 and 1665, either as a defending counsel or as a prosecutor.

An interesting tale[5] survives from the time when Turner was a resident of Lincoln's Inn. On Friday, 3 July 1640, Turner was drinking in the 'Three Cranes' in Chancery Lane with five companions, when John Skelton, one of a group in an adjoining room,

LYDE GREEN, HOLDSHOTT with a view of the boggy ground
'Where my father dwells, adjoyning the . . . Grove'. (Turner *Botanologia* p. 274)
No trace of the house exists today   *Photograph R. E. Cousins*

accused the six of throwing wine into his room. They retaliated by
throwing a glass of wine over the heads of Skelton and one of his
friends, after which a fight developed. Stephen Holyer, a friend of
Skelton, claimed that Turner's group called for a 'pottle of sack' and
forced them to drink the health of the traitorous Archbishop of
Canterbury, William Laud.[6] Holyer's cloak was then given to the
vintner's wife to pay for the bill and he was carried to a pump and

doused in water. This was followed by a beating, but Turner and his friends denied Holyer's accusations and said that he willingly left his cloak for payment. Their version of the event was verified by Thomas Tapping, the vintner's servant, although the notorious toast apparently did occur. After the Lords had read an affidavit sworn by Skelton and Holyer complaining of the 'unprovoked' attack, an Order in Council was issued on 17 July demanding that Turner and his friends account for themselves. The matter was dropped, however, since the testimonies of Turner, four of his companions, and the vintner's boy outnumbered those of their accusers.

Between 1640 and the publication of Turner's first book, ΜΙΚΡΟΚΟΣΜΟΣ. *A Description of the Little World, Being a Discovery of the Body of Man* [Mikrokosmos], in 1654, virtually nothing is known of his activities. At some point he lived in Wokingham[7] and his early interest in astrological herbalism is evidenced, when he wrote that, in 1644, he had 'taken water out of a hollow beech in Bramsil Park in Hampshire, which has cured the Itch'.[8] Later Turner may have entered domestic service, for when a certain 'William Allen, late of Grimston, Norfolk, but now of London', died in March 1647, he bequeathed

> to my worthy friend and kinsman Sir John Thorowgood my diamond ring and to his good lady and wife the picture in my chamber . . . To Robert Turner, a servant to Sir John Thorowgood, one black suit of clothes and boots.[9]

Possibly a different Robert Turner; but, Turner did dedicate the *Mikrokosmos* to the 'Lady Thorowgood, wife of the Right Woshipfull, Sir John Thorowgood of Kensington . . . for your manifold and extraordinary favours and curtesies exhibited towards me in both sickness and health'. He begs her to 'pardon his boldness in this and command me in what liberal service you please'. The somewhat obsequious nature of the dedication may reflect that Turner had once been a servant of the Thorowgoods, while the coincidence of the names certainly supports this possibility.

Diabolical Sorceries

By the mid-1650s, Turner was living in Carpenter's Yard, which was not far from Christopher Alley, where he eventually dwelt. The yard was to the south of Little Britain, with a passage to the Town Ditch, a covered sewer. The yard was possibly located in the northern part of Christ's Hospital, which had been founded in 1553 as a school for orphans. The Hospital complex, a crowded site of 'courts, yards and places', consisted of the old buildings of the former Greyfriars

Monastery (dissolved 1538) and included Christ Church, the parish church. Only the southern half was occupied by the institution, the northern section being leased to tenants, such as Robert Turner, in order to increase the Hospital revenues. Little Britain was well-known in the seventeenth century for its printing offices and booksellers and this would have been useful to Turner, who was then at his literary peak. The area was largely destroyed in the Great Fire of 1666 and, today, the site of Carpenter's Yard is occupied by King Edward Street. The Hospital was rebuilt by Wren, but later demolished to make way for the General Post Office.

During the Civil War and the Commonwealth (1642–1660), an end was seen to the stranglehold of the Church over the land. Ecclesiastical censorship ceased as did Church control over education and this resulted in greater intellectual freedom. Sects, hitherto illegal, met and discussed their views in public and it became much easier to write and publish on formerly taboo subjects. The publication of Turner's translations of Agrippa, Paracelsus and 'Solomon' would not have been possible during Laud's reign of terror and he could have been charged with witchcraft. In fact, such was the revival of hermeticism in the 1650s that more magical and alchemical books were published at this time than in the whole of the previous century.

The intellectual climate was thus an inspiration to Turner's Renaissance spirit. He translated and annotated the early texts for the advancement of learning and for the enlightenment of the general public. In the introduction to *Astrologicall Opticks* (1655) he explains that the works of 'Antient' authors are 'scarce to be had in the originall'. He had translated the book, so that it could be 'revived to see the light again' and not 'dye in obscurity'. The book concerned was *Astrolabium Planum* (1488), which had been compiled in Augsburg by Johann Engel or Angelus (1472–1512) and later reprinted in Venice in 1494. Similarly, in his translation of Paracelsus's *Of the Chymical Transmutation, Genealogy and Generation of Metals and Minerals* (1657), he writes: 'I revived them [these treatises] to posterity, hoping there may yet come a thankful age, in which learning may see Halcyon dayes.' The book had been originally published in Latin in 1576. Bound with the translation was a little work by another of Dee's favourite philosophers, Ramon Lull, entitled *Philosophical and Chymical Experiments of that famous Philosopher Raymond Lully; containing the right and due composition of both Elixirs [and] the admirable and perfect way of making the great Stone of the Philosophers.* Turner was assisted with his translation by a mysterious 'W. W., Student in the Celestial Sciences'.

Most of Turner's publications contain an *Address to the Reader* or an introduction in which he describes the object of the work and tries to dispel popular misconceptions. The introductions are invariably provocative, especially in the works dealing with the occult. He endeavours to educate people to distinguish between high magic, which has evolved from 'God and the Cosmos', and base witchcraft, sorcery and superstition. Today, some three hundred years later, the distinction still remains unclear in the minds of many people. To make his point he often deliberately insults the reader, but rapidly apologises to those who are outside of his attacks. For example, in the preface to his translation of Agrippa's *Fourth Book* Turner states that

> Magick itself, which the ancients did so divinely contemplate, is scandalized with bearing the badg of all diabolical sorceries . . . and as dogges barke at those they know not: so doe many condemne and hate things they understand not . . . Magicke and Witchcraft are far differing Sciences.

He expected some

> calumnies and obtrecations against this, from the malicious prejudiced man, and the lazie affecters of Ignorance, of whom this age swarms . . . But I incite the Reader to a charitable opinion hereof. . .And if there be any scandal in this enterprise of mine, it is taken, not given.

Readers are divided into four categories, namely

> Spunges, which attract all without distinguishing; Hour-glasses, which receive, and pour out as fast; Bags, which retain onely the dregs of Spices, and let the Wine escape; and Sieves, which retain the best onely.

He presents the *Fourth Book* to the last group 'knowing that they may reap good thereby'.

Similarly, in *Astrologicall Opticks*, Turner contributed a long introductory diatribe against the ignorance and superstition of the 'Vulgar People', who were frightened by

> those Raw-heads and Bloody-bones, where-with Mothers use to scare their Children from running abroad.

Moreover, the ignorant believed all old women to be witches, who made pacts with the Devil and rode

> up and down in the Aire with him; [and danced] abroad like Cats while their Bodies have lain as dead by their Husbands.

As a result of believing these 'idle stories', the people had, in fact, the Devil as a tutor. To counteract this superstition, Turner had a simple remedy which is still pertinent today.

> Let every one learne to know himselfe and keepe the Devill out of his own bosome and he need not feare him any where else.

One year later in his translation of Paracelsus's *Of the Supreme Mysteries of Nature* (1656), Turner defines the Devil for the benefit of the 'ignorant', because their 'Priests that should teach them knowledge, either cannot or else will not'.

> As in the Microcosmos or little world Man, the Soul is the best part, and the excrement the worst; so in the great world, as the Universal creating Spirit is the best part, so is the Devil the excrement of that Universal Spirit.

The book formed part of the *Archidoxes Magicae* of Paracelsus which had been published in Latin at Cracow in 1569.

The *Ars Notoria: the Notary Art of Solomon* (1657) conducted people further into the realms of the holy magician. In the introduction to this translation, Turner told the 'ingenious reader' that the book's 'virtues will soon be known, if practised, and the blasts of vice dispersed'.

The *Ars Notoria* and the *Lemegeton*

The Ars Notoria, the magical art of memory, flourished during the Middle Ages, although its origins are attributed to Solomon and Apollonius of Tyana. It was a process by which the magician could instantly gain knowledge or memory of all the arts and sciences. Each branch of knowledge or subject area was assigned a set of magical seals and characters, known as *notae*. To set the process into operation, the appropriate *notae* were contemplated whilst reciting angelic names and magical orisons. However, it was regarded as a diabolical form of magic, since the knowledge was quickly acquired from 'demons' without honest study. As a consequence, the Art was condemned by Thomas Aquinus (*c.* 1225–1274) and subsequent orthodox authorities. Nevertheless, in the sixteenth century, treatises on improving the memory were in demand, whether or not they were linked with works of necromancy and divination. Dee possessed two manuscript copies of the *Ars Notoria* and Simon Forman (1552–1611) records in his diary that in 1600 he 'wrote out the two bockes of "De Arte Memoratus" of Apollonius Niger, drawen with gould, of the seven liberal sciences'.[10] Robert Fludd (1574–1637) also encountered the *Ars Notoria* while in Toulouse during his European travels between 1600 and 1605. Turner's translation is based on a sixteenth-century Latin manuscript (Ashmole 5151) 'which Apollonius calleth "The Golden Flowers" . . . and this is Confirmed. Composed and Approved by the Authority of Solomon'.

The importance of the *Ars Notoria* has declined somewhat over the past two hundred years, owing to its association with the spurious grimoire of the *Lemegeton: The Lesser Key of Solomon*, a seventeenth-century compilation of five independent 'Solomonic' magical writings united by a descriptive title-page. The *Lemegeton* consists of *Goetia: the Book of Evil Spirits*, *Theurgia-Goetia*, the *Pauline Art*, the *Art Almadel*, and the *Ars Notoria*. It was probably compiled by an anonymous occultist who wished to assemble the lesser works attributed to Solomon into one convenient volume.

Twentieth-century occultists, such as A. E. Waite, have seen fit to distort the facts surrounding the composition of the *Lemegeton*, extolling the work as a legendary grimoire and overlooking the earlier independent existence of its individual parts. The Elizabethan magi knew nothing of the *Lemegeton*, but they were familiar with the contents. A form of the *Goetia*, for example, had appeared in Latin as the *Pseudomonarchia Daemonum* in Johann Wier's *De Praestigiis Daemonum* which was published in Basel in 1563. The *Pseudomonarchia* was later translated into English by T. R. in 1570 and printed in Reginald Scot's *Discouerie of Witchcraft* (1584). As the warden of Christ's College, Manchester between 1596 and 1605, Dee often had to act as an adviser about cases of witchcraft and Wier's book was one of the works he consulted or lent to investigators.

Similarly, the *Theurgia-Goetia* is a version of the first book of the *Steganographia* of Johannes Trithemius, Abbot of Sponheim (1462–1516), which was written in 1500, while the third book of the *Lemegeton*, the *Pauline Art*, forms part of a sixteenth-century Latin manuscript in the Bibliothèque Nationale (BN 7170A). The Pauline Art itself was supposedly discovered by the Apostle Paul and delivered by him at Corinth. Likewise, the *Art Almadel*, which deals with the spirits of the Four Altitudes, can be found in a fifteenth-century manuscript in Florence (Florence II-iii-24). By the sixteenth century, both the Pauline Art and the Art Almadel, like the Ars Notoria, had been condemned as sinful and superstitious magic. The early history of the fifth book, the *Ars Notoria*, has been discussed.

Sloane Manuscripts 2731 and 3648 are the main sources of the *Lemegeton*, although the *Ars Notoria* is omitted from Sloane 2731. Nevertheless, the *Ars Notoria* of the 'complete' Sloane 3648 is none other than an ink-blotted and often illegible transcript of Robert Turner's published translation of 1657. The manuscript is, in fact, a rendering of an untraceable manuscript compiled in 1640/1, a fact determined by the inclusion of the Angels of the Hours of the Day and Night for Wednesday, 10 March 1641, as an example of the daily angelic calculations required for the *Pauline Art*. The original compilation of the *Lemegeton*, therefore, was made too early for the inclusion of Turner's translation of the *Ars Notoria*. This was added to Sloane 3648, probably for the benefit of the transcriber, along with sections from the *Archidoxes Magicae* of Paracelsus (not Turner's translation) and scraps from the English translation of Book Two of Agrippa's *Occult Philosophy* (1651).

Sloane 2731 was commenced on 18 January 1687[11] and was a later attempt to produce a neat transcript from more than one manuscript of the *Lemegeton*, including Sloane 3648 and possibly the mysterious work of 1640/1. Variations in the names of the Goetic spirits are noted in the margins and all derive from Sloane 3648. Turner's *Ars Notoria* was omitted from Sloane 2731, possibly because it was still available from booksellers and also because this part of Sloane 3648 is particularly illegible. The *Lemegeton* manuscripts, therefore, are useful compilations of early grimoires, adapted to suit the requirements of individual seventeenth-century magicians, rather than copies of a medieval comprehensive grimoire.

A recent attempt[12] to publish the complete *Lemegeton* of Sloane 3648 for the first time was marred by crudely drawn illustrations and the omission of the *Ars Notoria*, which was condemned as 'literary tripe' by the editor, who failed to understand the significance of the magical art of memory.

> Glorify thy Holy and unspeakable Name this day in my heart, and strengthen my intellectual understanding; increase my memory, and confirm my eloquence; make my tongue ready, quick, and perfect in thy Sciences and Scriptures, that by thy power given unto me, and thy wisdom taught in my heart, I may praise thee, and know and understand thy Holy Name.[13]

Fortunately, the omission was offset, when a new American reprint of Turner's translation was published in 1987.

Transition

Robert Turner's opinions were well-respected. He associated with a circle of well-known contemporary astrologers, such as William Lilly (1602–1681), Doctor Nicholas Fiske, (1573–1659?) and the latter's pupil, John Gadbury (1627–1704), who had drawn a natal chart for Culpeper. These astrologers, along with several Cambridge scholars, wrote commendary epistles and poems which were printed at the beginning of Turner's works. For instance, Lilly wrote in *Astrologicall Opticks* that Turner 'hath very well translated it and delivered the Astrological sense of every sentence judiciously'. Similar compliments were not uncommon in Turner's books. Lilly, incidentally, had fruitlessly endeavoured to discover buried treasure in the cloisters of Westminster Abbey in 1634, using the magical circle and invocatory methods detailed in a Latin manuscript copy of the *Ars Notoria*.

Turner himself often dedicated his works to colleagues from Christ's College and to friends, such as the notorious quack or 'Empiricus Famosus', Doctor Trigge of Tower Wharf, who invented the worthless Golden Vatican Pills which allegedly cured all diseases. The landed gentry were also honoured, including the aforementioned Lady Thorowgood; Mrs Elizabeth Creswell, widow of Thomas Creswell, whose family had owned the Manor of Heckfield since the fifteenth century; and Sir William Pitt of Stratfield Saye, Hampshire.

Pitt was complimented with *Sal, Lumen et Spiritus Mundi Philosophici* (1657) which was one of Turner's final alchemical translations. The book had been written originally in French by Clovis Hesteau, Sieur de Nuysement, at the turn of the seventeenth century. Turner translated the 1651 Latin edition of Ludwig Combach of Hesse (1590–1657). The purpose of publishing this 'piece of Hermetical Philosophy which is well-seasoned with Salt' was to provide information on the Salt of the Philosophers, the third of the Three Alchemical Principles, which form the primal stage of manifestation. Turner believed sufficient had been published on Mercury and Sulphur, the two other Principles of Nature, and hoped that this work would restore the balance. For the 'intelligent and deserving' the book would be a 'great revealed secret', but not so for those 'degenerate bastards . . . not a whit tinctured with the Salt of the Philosophers'.

With the advent of the Restoration in 1660, the ecclesiastical hierarchy returned and the Church gained more power. Dissenters found themselves excluded from State office and university, and in this atmosphere there was not the same freedom to publish works on magic. The publication of Meric Casaubon's *A True and Faithful Relation of what passed for many Years between Dr John Dee . . . and some Spirits* in 1659 had already helped to create a reaction against occultism. Casaubon deliberately set out to discredit Dee and his contemporary followers, so that he (Casaubon) could promote religion and refute charges of atheism which had been levelled against him. He succeeded only too well. Dee's maligned reputation as the dupe of Edward Kelly and as a foolish conjuror of angels stemmed from Casaubon and lasted well into the twentieth century.

The Licensing Act of 1663 kept a close watch on the press, in order to prevent the publication of 'heretical' works. The Act ensured that books could not be published without prior consultation with the

Church or State. At the same time, the number of master printers in the country were reduced to twenty. As a consequence, Turner was forced to abandon the translation of further occult treatises. He concentrated instead upon his interest in medicine and the Doctrine of Signatures, which fortunately proved successful for him.

By 1657 he had already published four medical books, including translations of two sixteenth-century works, the *Compleat Bone-Setter* (1656) of Thomas Moulton (fl. 1540?), a self-styled 'Doctor of Divinity of the Order of Friar Preachers', and the *Enchiridion Medicum* (1657), both of which he substantially enlarged. The latter work formed the English translation of *Praxis Medicorum* by John Sadler, who had died in 1595. Turner was also the author of the curiously entitled *The Woman's Counsellor, or the Feminine Physician, modestly treating of such occult accidents and secret diseases incident to that sex* (1657?), in which he displays a rare concern for women and their problems. The world of writing and publishing was a male domain at that time with most published works reflecting this, and so it was unusual for a man to produce a book sympathetic to women. Turner writes in *Of the Chymical Transmutation* that he hoped the *Women's Counsellor* would enable women to become their 'own helpers in such private infirmities, as too much modesty they oft-times to their own hurt conceal'.

The *Botanologia* and the Doctrine of Signatures

In March 1663, Turner completed his *magnum opus*, the comprehensive and astrological herbal, ΒΟΤΑΝΟΛΟΓΙΑ. *The Brittish Physician; or, the Nature and Vertues of English Plants*. As the subject matter could hardly rate as dangerous occultism, its publication was guaranteed. The book was published in 1664 and was his first work for seven years. Turner used Holdshott as an occasional base for his field studies, since several herbs are noted as growing in his father's garden or elsewhere in the neighbourhood.

The *Botanologia* was based on the Doctrine of Signatures, in which Turner was a firm believer. The Doctrine had a strong following during the sixteenth and seventeenth centuries and had been popularised by Paracelsus (1483–1541), who had expanded the ancient belief for guidance in selecting herbal remedies to cure the ailments of his patients. According to this dogma, every plant bore a 'signature' of its medical application. In the *Botanologia*, Turner wrote that 'God hath imprinted upon the Plants, Herbs and Flowers, as it were in Hieroglyphicks, the very Signature of their Vertues'. Plants could resemble the part of the body or the ailment which they could cure. For example, walnuts could treat diseases of the brain, to which the kernel was likened, while plants with a yellow sap were good for jaundice. Signatures also represented dangerous animals. The plants in this case would act as an antidote. Hence Adder's Tongue cured the bite of the Adder. Some herbs, however, were left blank in order to encourage people to find the appropriate properties for themselves. In addition, herbs were placed under the dominion of one of the five planets, the Sun or the Moon, together with a sign of the Zodiac. Different parts of the body, moreover, were governed by similar astrological influences. Diseases were felt to be caused by particular planets and could be healed by a herb of the opposing planet. In this way an illness produced by Jupiter was curable by a herb under the sovereignty of Mercury. Alternatively, the malady could be cured 'sympathetically' by employing plants belonging to the planet causing the disease. These particular aspects of the Doctrine of Signatures were reflected in Turner's first book, *Mikrokosmos*, which included sections on the 'sicknesses attributed to the twelve Signes and Planets, with their Natures'.

In England the Doctrine had been promoted by Turner's contemporary, Nicholas Culpeper, with his herbal, *The English Physician Enlarged, with 369 Medicines made of English Herbs*. Published in 1653 and still in demand today, the book was written in a language which appealed to the ordinary person. Turner's *Botanologia. The Brittish Physician*, which deliberately aped the title of Culpeper's book, unfortunately remained forever in the shadow of that work with which it could never compete. After its initial publication, the *Botanologia* was sufficiently successful to be reprinted in 1687, but it is now forgotten.

The *Botanologia* presented the means whereby 'people may gather their own Physick under every Hedge, or in their Gardens . . .; so that . . . they may become their own Physicians'. Almost five hundred herbs, plants and spices are described alphabetically, together with their properties and astrological government. A table of diseases with their herbal cures is appended. Nevertheless, the reader is warned not to abuse the plants by making sacrifices to them and uttering charms over them like the 'Cacochymists, Medean Hags and Sorcerers now adays; who . . . out of some Diabolical intention search after the more Magical and Occult Vertues of Herbs and Plants to accomplish some wickedness'.

Turner respects the discoveries of pioneer Elizabethan herbalist, John Gerard (1545–1607); but Culpeper, whom Turner considered a serious rival, is insulted throughout the *Botanologia*. 'Culpeper teacheth how to kill serpents with [Alkanet] . . . but this is as ridiculous as Culpeper himself', who was obviously 'beside the saddle' when attributing Dodder of Thyme to Saturn. 'I am sure his logick is false', attacked Turner; but Culpeper had died of tuberculosis in 1654 and was unable to reply.

Herbalism versus the Plague

In 1665 Turner produced a new edition of the *Compleat Bone-Setter*, which proved to be his final work and the last published in his lifetime. The book bore little relation to Moulton's original and included a portrait of Turner and a section on '*Treating the Pestilence*'. Just as osteopathy is disapproved of by the medical profession today, bone-setting was regarded as charlatanry by the College of Physicians, the seventeenth-century medical authorities, because the skill was considered hereditary and instinctual and not scientifically acquired. Nevertheless, with the panic and desperation caused by the plague, which had begun in the first week of June 1665, any book on self-help was welcome. The book was dated 25 June 1665 and was, therefore, well-timed, particularly as Turner himself was running short of funds. He had been forced to transfer a prosecution to a Mr Peck through lack of money, so revenue from the sale of the book would have been helpful. The book would have been particularly appealing, for Turner was at pains to write in 'plain English', as he states in the introduction, so that 'people who are able, may easily make medicines for themselves'.

The *Compleat Bone-Setter* extensively advertised Turner's sideline in medical remedies. Various treatments are listed which were available from his house in Christopher Alley or from his bookseller, Thomas Rooks, at the Lamb and Ink-Bottle at the east-end of St Paul's. Regrettably, some of the remedies ring of quackery and possibly Turner, like many others, may have been capitalising on the general ill health of the plague-stricken city. His most exotic remedy was the 'Sovereign Antidote against the Plague, and all infectious Diseases, Foggie and unhealthy Airs, Essex and Kentish Agues'. This was sold by Rooks along with the *Ars Notoria* and the *Fourth Book*, and an 'excellent powder to procure easie delivery in Child-bearing women'. From his house, Turner sold a 'Balsam for Sore Eyes, and for preservation of the Sight' and his 'Approved Dentifrices for cleansing the Teeth'. The book itself included several remedies and treatments for all stages of the plague. Before going 'abroad out of thy house' it was recommended to drink nine spoonfuls of white wine in a saucer of vinegar. Roses, camphor, cinnamon, mace, nutmeg, amber, citron peel and musk could be mixed with red storax and laudanum to provide a pomander, while another protective antiseptic drink demanded a spoonful of beaten gunpowder stirred into six spoonfuls of Aqua Vitae.[14]

Unfortunately, the 'Sovereign Antidote' and the other remedies did not work for Turner himself. The DNB speculation that he was a victim of the plague is most probably correct. His name is mentioned for the last time in the *Calendar of State Papers* during June 1665. No further publications appeared, apart from reprints of the *Woman's Counsellor* in 1686 and the *Botanologia* in 1687. The latter includes the whole of the 1664 introduction, but the date is omitted, and the accompanying portrait of Turner is a copy of the *Compleat Bone-Setter* portrait.

The City of London was severely afflicted by the plague. Nearly 1200 people died in the City during the week of 12 September 1665, and 48 of these were buried in Christ Church, the parish in which Turner lived. If the plague was indeed his fate, he probably suffered an anonymous burial in one of the communal graves for plague victims.

The Loss of the *Steganographia* of Trithemius

Before the Restoration curtailed his occult studies, Robert Turner had planned to produce English translations of the remainder of the *Archidoxes Magicae* of Paracelsus, Agrippa's *Occult Philosophy*, and the *Steganographia* of Trithemius. In the introduction to *Of the Supreme Mysteries of Nature*, Turner writes:

> Shortly expect (*Deo volente*) the other parts [of Paracelsus] hereof, and some comments on this and them, together with the famous art of Steganography, *Authore Tritemio*, to speak our own Language; and perhaps the Occult Philosophy of Agrippa digested into a plainer method.

Sadly, his early death meant that the work was never completed, if even commenced, with resultant loss to occult scholarship.

Agrippa and Paracelsus were supposedly pupils of Johannes Trithemius and together the three exercised considerable influence upon the magical tradition of England and Europe during the sixteenth and seventeenth centuries. Both Dee and Simon Forman considered the *Steganographia* an important instructional source on Cabalistic Angel Magic. Forman recorded in his diary that he had made a copy of the four books of the *Steganographia* in the year 1600, while Dee obtained a manuscript copy much earlier in 1562, during a visit to Antwerp. On 16 February 1563, Dee excitedly wrote to Sir William Cecil about the acquisition.

> I have purchased on boke, for which a Thowsand Crownes have ben by others offred, and yet could not be obteyned. A boke,

for which many a lerned man hath long sowght, and dayly yet doth seeke: Whose use is greater than the fame thereof is spread: the name thereof to you is not unknowne: The title is on this wise, Steganographia Joannis Tritemij . . . Of this Boke the one half (with contynuall Labor and watch, the most part of X days) have I copyed oute.[15]

The *Steganographia* consists of three books with a *Clavis Steganographia* or 'Special Key' to the operations detailed in the first three volumes. Together these constituted the four books which Forman copied. The first book was completed on 27 March 1500 and, throughout the sixteenth century, the whole work secretly circulated in manuscript form, until it was published in Frankfurt in 1606. Complete editions of the *Steganographia* were readily available when Robert Turner was planning his translation, but unfortunately this is no longer the case. A recent translation[16] omits the second book and the key, as these volumes are believed lost. Had Turner's translation been available, the work could have been studied more thoroughly over the past 300 years, with reprints presenting little problem.

The *Steganographia* was undoubtedly the inspiration for Agrippa's *Occult Philosophy*, which was published in Cologne in 1533. The book was much studied by Dee, who had two copies in his library. In 1510 Agrippa visited Trithemius at his abbey at Sponheim near Mainz and presented the Abbot with the first draft of the *Occult Philosophy*. It was translated into English by John French (1616?–1657)[17] and published in 1651, but Turner evidently felt that he could improve upon this translation. Nevertheless, this was not to be. In the same address to the reader in which he writes of his future plans, Robert Turner apologises for a delay in producing a new translation of Agrippa with a doom-laden quote from Ovid's *Metamorphoses*, strangely prophetic of the forthcoming troubles of the 1660s.

NUBILA SUNT SUBITIS TEMPORA NOSTRA MALIS

'Our times are suddenly clouded with evil' – and for Robert Turner regrettably they were.

Robert Turner of 'Holshott': Published Works

Original Writings

[Botanologia] Βοτανολογια. The Brittish Physician; or, The Nature and Vertues of English Plants, London, 1664.

[Botanologia], London, 1687.

Reprint of 1664 edition with portrait.

[Mikrokosmos] Μικροκοσμος. *A Description of the Little-World, being a discovery of the Body of Man exactly delineating all the members, bones, veins, sinews, arteries, and parts thereof, from the head to the foot. Hereunto is added . . . the cure of wounds . . . the sicknesses attributed to the twelve Signes and Planets, with their Natures,* London, 1654.

Woman's Counsellor, or the Feminine Physician, modestly treating of such occult accidents and secret diseases incident to that sex, London [1657?]. Sold by Nathaniel Brook at the Angel in Cornhill.

Woman's Counsellor, or the Feminine Physician, London, 1686. Reprint of first edition.

Translations

Arbatel of Magick, de Magia Veterum, 1655. Bound with the *Fourth Book.*

Arabatel of Magick, 2nd edn, Gillette, New Jersey, 1979.

Archidoxes of Magic, by Paracelsus, London, 1975. 2nd edn of *Of the Supreme Mysteries of Nature.*

Ars Notoria: The Notary Art of Solomon; shewing the Cabalistic key of magical operations, the liberal sciences, divine revelation, and the art of memory. Whereunto is added an Astrological Catechism, fully demonstrating the art of Judicial Astrology. Written originally in Latine by Apollonius, Leovitius and others, and now Englished by R. Turner. London, 1657.

Ars Notoria: The Notary Art of Solomon. 2nd edn, Seattle, Washington, 1987. Omits Turner's introduction of 1657.

An Astrological Catechisme, wherein the Art of Judicial Astrology is fully demonstrated by way of Q. and A. Tr. out of Leovitius and revised by Robert Turner, 1657. Bound with the *Ars Notoria.*

Astrologicall Opticks. Wherein are represented the Faces of every Signe, with the Images of each Degree in the Zodiack; by Johannes Angelus [Johann Engel]. London, 1655.

Astronomical Geomancy; by Gerard of Cremona, 1655. Bound with the *Fourth Book.*

Compleat Bone-Setter: Being the Method of Curing Broken Bones, Dislocated Joynts, and Ruptures, commonly called Broken Bellies. Written originally by Friar [Thomas] Moulton; Englished and enlarged by Robert Turner. London, 1656.

Compleat Bone-Setter. 2nd edn, London, 1665. Includes portrait which was redrawn for the 1687 reprint of the *Botanologia.*

Compleat Bone-Setter. Isleworth, Middlesex: Tamor Pierston, 1981. Forty-eight-page facsimile of parts of the 1656 edition.

Enchiridion Medicum: An Enchiridion of the Art of Physick Methodically prescribing Remedies . . . to the Sick-Man . . . Containing a salubrious remedy for every malady incident to the body of Man. Written in Latin by our learned countryman John Sadler, Doctor in Physick; tr., revised, corrected and augmented by R. Turner. London, 1657.

Fourth Book of Occult Philosophy; attributed to Henry Cornelius Agrippa. London, 1655.

Fourth Book of Occult Philosophy. 2nd edn, London, 1978.

Heptameron: or, Magical Elements; ascribed to Peter de Abano. 1655. Bound with the *Fourth Book.*

Isagoge . . . Of the Nature of Spirits; by Georg Pictorius von Villingen, 1655. Bound with the *Fourth Book.*

Of the Chymical Transmutation, Genealogy, and Generation of Metals and Minerals, by Paracelsus, London, 1657.

Of Geomancy; attributed to Henry Cornelius Agrippa, 1655. Bound with the *Fourth Book.*

Of the Supreme Mysteries of Nature, by Paracelsus. Englished by R. Turner, London, 1656.

Philosophical and Chymical Experiments of that famous Philosopher Raymond Lully; containing the right and due Composition of both Elixirs; the admirable and perfect way of making the great Stone of the Philosophers . . . Now for the benefit of all lovers of Art and Knowledge, carefully translated out of High German and Latin, by W. W., student in the Celestial Sciences, and R. T. 1657. Bound with *Of the Chymical Transmutation.*

Sal, Lumen et Spiritus Mundi Philosophici: or, the dawning of the Day, discovered by the beams of light: shewing, the true salt and secrets of the philosophers, the first and universal Spirit of the World. Written originally in French by Clovis Hesteau, Sieur de Nuysement and afterwards turned into Latin by the illustrious Doctor Lodovicus Combachius [Ludwig Combach] and now transplanted into Albyons Garden by R. T. London, 1657.

Notes

1   *Book of Ceremonial Magic* (1911).
2   Christopher Alley ran west from St Martins-le-Grand and was the third on the left from Newgate Street. The area was destroyed in the Great Fire in 1666 and today the site is occupied by the General Post Office.
3   *Botanologia*, p. 124.
4   *Calendar of State Papers, Domestic, 1665*, p. 426.
5   *Calendar of State Papers, Domestic, 1640*, pp. 487, 504–5.
6   Laud (1573–1645) was a religious advisor to Charles I. As Archbishop from 1633 onwards, he persecuted Puritans wholesale and his policies were a major cause of the Civil War. In 1640 he was accused of treason, committed to the Tower, and finally beheaded in 1645.
7   '. . . a place I once lived in', *Botanologia*, p. 214.
8   Ibid., p. 34. Today, Bramsil Park is Bramshill Plantation, Forestry Commission land north-west of Heckfield.

9   Henry F. Waters, *Genealogical Gleanings in England*. New England Historic Genealogical Society, Boston, 1901, p. 602.

10   *Autobiography and Personal Diaries of Dr Simon Forman, the Celebrated Astrologer* ed. James Orchard Halliwell, 1849, p. 30.

11   Waite misread this date as 10 January 1676, which has been mistakenly quoted ever since.

12   *The Lemegetton: a Manual of Medieval Magic*, ed. Kevin Wilby. Silian, Dyfed: Hermetic Research Series, 1985.

13   *Ars Notoria*, tr. R. Turner, Seattle, 1987, p.45.

14   *Compleat Bone-Setter* (1665), pp. 142–7.

15   As transcribed by J. E. Bailey in *John Dee and Trithemius's 'Steganography'*, *Notes and Queries*, May 1879, pp. 401–2.

16   *The Steganographia of Johannes Trithemius*, tr. Fiona Tait and Christopher Upton, Magnum Opus Hermetic Sourceworks, Edinburgh, 1982.

17   French was an army physician and the author of the alchemical work, *The Art of Distillation* (1651).

Edw: Kelly *Prophet or Seer to D.ʳ Dee.*

EDWARD KELLY 1555–1595

Appendix A
Edward Kelly
Seer, Conjuror and Alchemist

The early life and movements of Edward Kelly[1] provide a subject worthy of further research. Of this man who exerted such a powerful influence over the learned Dr John Dee and fostered an occult tradition which has survived to the present day, surprisingly little is known.

According to the account given in Anthony à Wood's *Athenae Oxoniensis* (1813) Kelly was born at Worcester on 1 August 1555. The name of his father remains unknown, but it is said that he was an apothecary and of sufficient means to send his son to Oxford. Strangely, there is no record of any Edward Kelly having entered the University at that time, but several young men were admitted under the name of Talbot. As we have seen, in the early spiritual diaries, Dee first uses the name Talbot to introduce the mysterious character who entered his service during 1582, and who shortly after changed his name to Kelly. The reason for the alias is unknown, but most commentators believe (perhaps with some justification) that Talbot adopted the name Kelly to escape involvement with the law.

It seems that, after some sort of trouble, Kelly left Oxford in a hurry and travelled to Lancaster. Here he fell foul of the authorities on the grounds of forgery, and for this crime he is said to have been pilloried and deprived of his ears. It seems unlikely, however, that Kelly in fact suffered the last of these punishments, as Dee would hardly have imperilled his position at Court and his scientific reputation by his association with one branded as a common criminal.

Kelly spent some time travelling in Wales where, we are informed, he came into possession of the 'Book of St Dunstan', an alchemical tract, and the two powders of projection; whereby metals could be transmuted to gold and silver. Dee often mentions the book and powders in his diaries, but I can find no record of their use.

On moving to London Kelly took up the post of secretary for Thomas Allen who was, it seems, a magician of some reputation. Dr Peter French suggests that Kelly may have acquired some of his occult knowledge while in Allen's employ.[2]

While at Lancaster he attempted to raise the dead in the churchyard of Walton le Dale. In his book *Ancient Funerall Monuments*, John Weever relates how Kelly and his companion Paul Waring dug up the corpse of a man recently buried and 'by their incantations . . . made him to speak . . . strange predictions'.

Although history marks Kelly as an impostor and scoundrel of the lowest morals, it is not easy to see how he would be able to convince Dee of his scrying abilities so fully if the Angelic messages were complete fabrication: Dee may not have been worldly-wise in all matters, but he was certainly not a fool. In addition the very nature of the 'received' material implies a standard of education, and a memory capacity, far beyond that possessed by Kelly. When one compares the content of the Englished angelic keys, with the literary style of Kelly's three alchemical works – *The Stone of the Philosophers, The Humid Way* and *The Theatre of Terrestrial Astronomy*[3] – there seems no doubt that a quite different personality is involved. Perhaps the spirits did speak through Kelly, or was it some hidden facet of his mind which emerged only during trance? Whatever the answer I feel sure that the scope, magnitude, and complexity of Dee's angel-magic rules out the involvement of simple trickery.

Finally, it seems that even the spirits did not always side with Kelly. He was ordered by the angel Michael to take a wife and shortly after reluctantly married Joan Cooper of Chipping Norton. From the outset the marriage proved to be a disaster and Kelly often told Dee that wedlock had been against his wishes and he hated his wife. Divine wrath!?

Although the Bohemian Emperor Rudolph II had earlier knighted Kelly for his alchemical works, he later lost patience with him as he failed to produce the promised gold. Kelly was arrested and confined in the dungeon of castle Zobeslau and later transferred to castle Zerner. At the request of Dee, Queen Elizabeth tried to secure Kelly's release, claiming him as her subject, but Rudolph refused to give the alchemist his liberty. All else failing, Kelly attempted to escape but, in so doing, fell from the castle turret and shortly after died from his injuries.

Kelly met his death in November 1595 in his fortieth year.

Notes

1   Sometimes the spelling *Kelley* is used. Dee uses both forms of the name in his diaries.
2   *John Dee, the World of an Elizabethan Magus*, P. J. French.
3   Published in *The Alchemical Writings of Edward Kelly*, London, 1970. Limited edition.

Appendix B
Explanatory Diagrams to Dee Texts

Notes

p. 156   *Sigillum Dei Aemeth*: (Sloane MS. 3188, fol. 30). John Dee's principal wax seal, used in conjunction with the Holy Table.

p. 157   *The Holy Table*: It will be noticed that the diagram reproduced here shows the characters in the borders and central square in the reverse order to that published by Casaubon in his *True and Faithful Relation*. The reason for this apparent transposition of the angelic characters is that, due to a block-maker's error, Casaubon's 1659 version was (it seems) accidentally printed in reverse. The version given here has been redrawn from Dee's Latin lettered example to be found in the Appendix of Sloane MS. 3188. Elias Ashmole examined the Table while it was in the Library of Sir John Cotton. He describes it as being made from fine-grained wood with a top measuring $36\frac{1}{4}$ inches by $35\frac{7}{8}$ inches and $\frac{7}{10}$ of an inch thick. The Table top was placed upon a frame two feet eight inches square, and two feet seven and a half inches high. The four legs of the Table were each three inches square. The frame of the Table had a wooden case incorporated 'closed with 3 Iron Hasps, to be locked up with 3 Padlocks'. The letters down each side of the table were painted on a gold background; the central square had blue lines and gold letters; the Hexagram was painted in gold lines, and the Seven Ensigns of Creation had blue lines and red characters. The whereabouts of the Table is now unknown (possibly destroyed in the Cottonian Library fire of 1731). A late seventeenth-century copy of the Table (in marble) may be seen in the Oxford Museum of the History of Science.

p. 158–9   *The Seven Ensigns of Creation*: The Angels first instructed that they should be made from purified tin, but later Dee was told to paint the emblems onto the Table.

p. 159   *The position of the Seven Ensigns on the Table*: The annexed numbers refer to the order in which the Ensigns appear in the present text.

p. 160   *The true Lamyne*: In Latin and Angelic characters.

p. 160   *Edward Kelly's Vision of the Four Castles*.

p. 161   *John Dee's Horoscope*: redrawn from a chart in his own hand (Sloane MS. 1782, fol. 31).

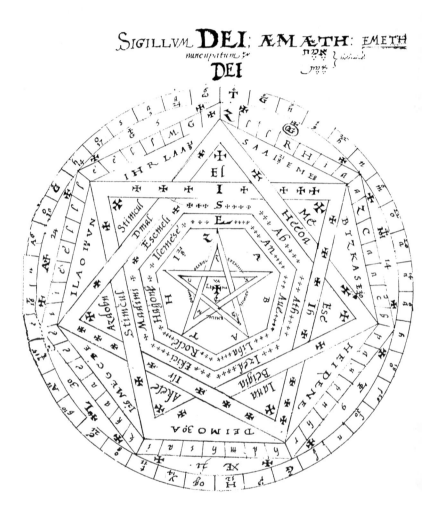

SIGILLUM DEI AEMETH Sloane MS. 3188 fol. 30
Courtesy British Library Board

THE HOLY TABLE

THE SEVEN ENSIGNS OF CREATION

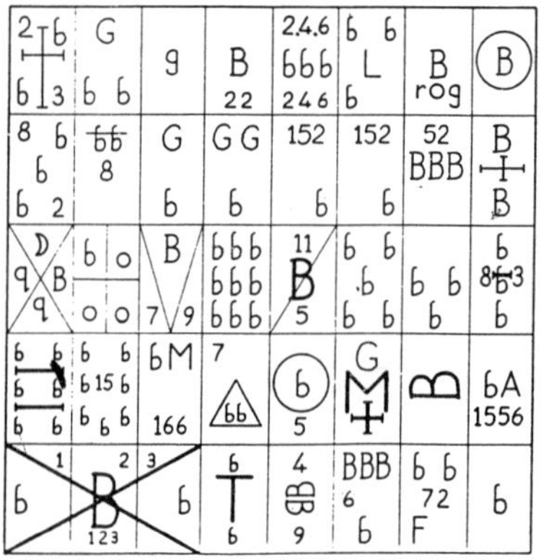

1.

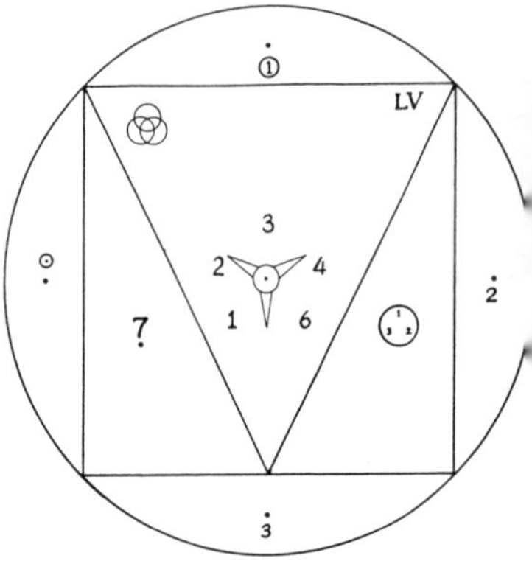

2.

3.

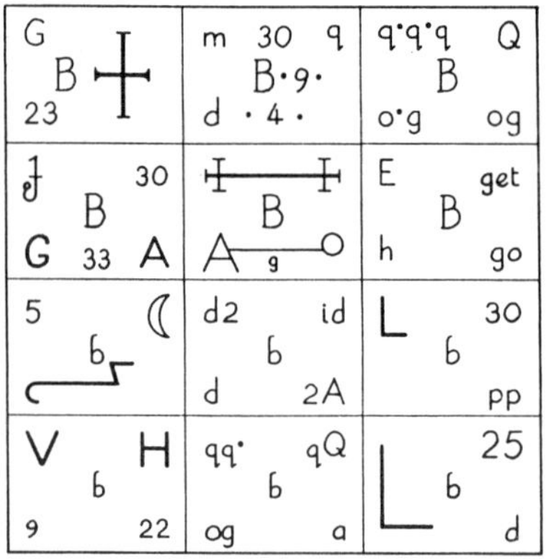

4.

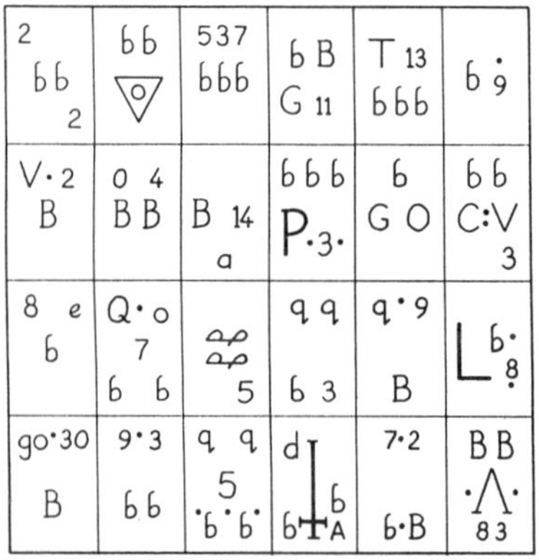

5.

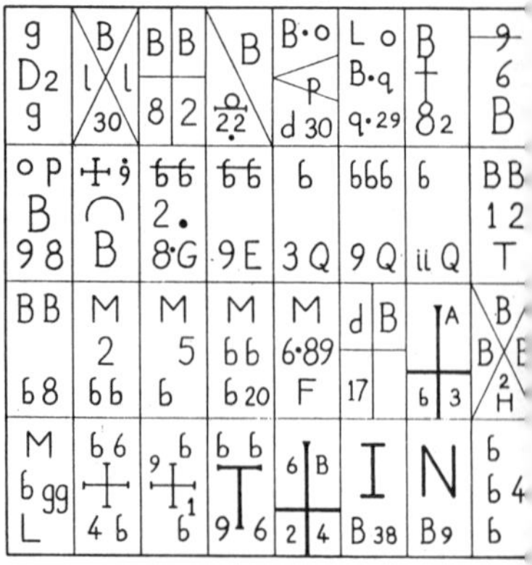

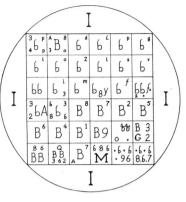

6.

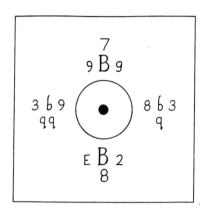

7.

THE POSITION OF THE SEVEN ENSIGNS ON THE TABLE

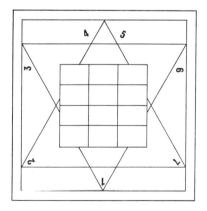

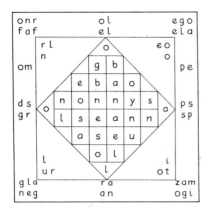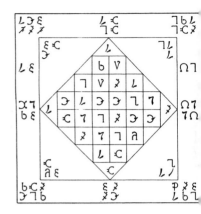

THE TRUE LAMYNE In Latin & Angelic Characters

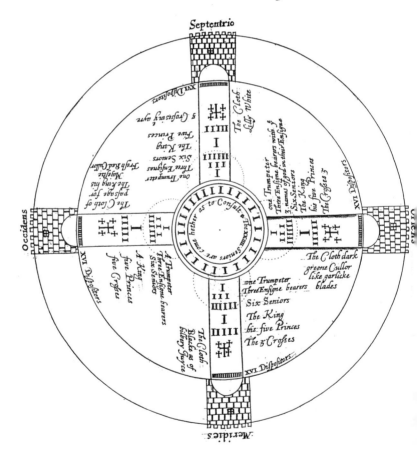

EDWARD KELLY'S VISION OF THE FOUR CASTLES

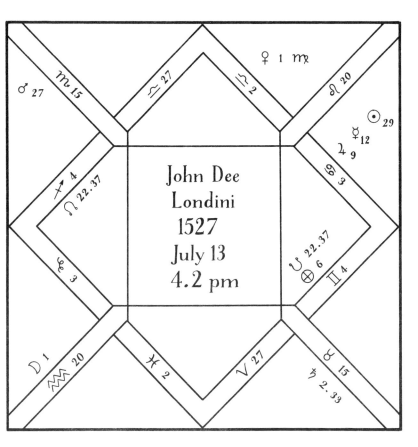

JOHN DEE'S HOROSCOPE

Appendix C
The Physical Location of the Ninety-One Parts of the Earth named by Man, as detailed in the *Liber Scientiae Auxilii et Victoriae Terrestris* of John Dee
by Robin E. Cousins

Liber Scientiae Auxillii et Victoriae Terrestris, which forms part of Sloane Manuscript 3191, provides the details necessary to operate a system of magic, by which the magician can discover

> how to compare . . . [the] divisions of provinces according to the Divisions of the Stars, with the Ministry of the Ruling Intelligences, and Blessings of the Tribes of Israel, the Lots of the Apostles, and Typical Seals of the Sacred Scripture, [so that he] shall be able to obtain great and prophetical oracles, concerning every region, of things to come.[1]

While in Cracow, John Dee and Edward Kelly received on Wednesday, 23 May 1584, the names of ninety-one regions and provinces of the physical world, as defined by man, from the spirit Nalvage. At this time America was no longer considered to be a group of islands; but Australia had yet to be discovered and the search for the North-West Passage had just commenced. The names of the ninety-one parts relate to the Ptolemaic ancient world of about AD 150 (see Map 8) with some additions. The Spirit Nalvage explains:

> Notwithstanding the Angel of the Lord appeared unto Ptolemie, and opened unto him the parts of the Earth: but some he was commanded to secret: and those are Northward under your Pole. But unto yon, the very true names of the World in her Creation are delivered.[2]

The list is not altogether satisfactory. Dee, who was well-versed in geography, had not heard of some of the places and even Nalvage said, 'Here are 15, which were never known in these times . . . The rest are.' Many of the strange locations are indeed in the polar regions, which were uncharted at the time. In fact, a considerable Arctic land mass was believed to exist and was featured on sixteenth-century maps (see Maps 5 and 6). Nevertheless, locations for this region are desirable and there are many areas in the extreme north, whether land or sea, which can be covered by the descriptions. The belief of a south polar continent (Tolpam, Part 58) was not inaccurate, a location which can usefully extend to Australasia which was undiscovered at the time (see Maps 5 and 7).

Two interesting points emerge at the end of the communication relating to known lands not included in the list. Firstly, when Dee asks of 'Polonia, Moschovia, Dania, Hibernia (Ireland), Islandia, and so of many others', Nalvage replies: 'Polonia and Moscovia, are of Sarmatia (Russia); Denmark, Ireland, Frizeland, Iseland, are of Britain: And so it is of the rest.'[3] Does this imply that Brytania (Part 61) can be used to gain access to lands not included within the ninety-one parts? Secondly, when Dee presses Nalvage as to which part governs 'Atlantis and the annexed places, under the King of Spain called the West Indies', Nalvage replies: 'When these 30 appear, they can each tell you what they own. Prepare for tomorrows Action.' The communication is, therefore, incomplete. Unfortunately, 'tomorrows Action' never occurred, because Kelly believed Nalvage to have taken the descriptions from books, including Agrippa's 'Occult Philosophy', and refused to communicate further. 'E. K. remained of his wilful intent', noted a frustrated Dee. However, Onigap (Part 34) may refer to these lands and there is always the use of Brytania, as described above. Note that Dee held that the term 'West Indies' was very misleading and preferred to use 'Atlantis' instead of 'America', as a name for the new lands. Nevertheless, the additional thirty parts wait to be realised, which would bring the total of the parts of the Earth to 121.

Dee bought Gerhard Mercator's *Universal Chart of the World* and the geographical work of Pomponius Mela to help him with his locations. He does not record his success. Ultimately, the advice of Nalvage in relation to Chaldei (Part 42) and Chaldea (Part 72) is the only way to establish the locations of the obscure and ambiguously described parts of the world: 'You shall finde the difference of it, in practice.'

The Ninety-One Parts of the World

Many of the locations are well-known. However, for the obscurer areas *A True and Faithful Relation* . . . is often the only guide and, in these instances, supportive quotations are given. Other parts, especially those located by Kelly or Nalvage in the Far Orient or in the Arctic regions, are difficult to place on the world map today, as in Dee's time these regions were largely unexplored and uncharted.

1   AEGYPTUS: Egypt.

2   SYRIA: Southern Syria.

3   MESOPOTAMIA: Land between the Tigris and Euphrates rivers in Northern Iraq and North-East Syria.

4   CAPPADOCIA: Extensive province of Central Turkey, stretching from the Black Sea in the north to Cilicia (Part 14) in the south. The original territory, Cappadocia Proper, occupied the southern areas.

5   TUSCIA: Tuscany or Etruria, a province in Central Italy including Florence.

6   PARVA ASIA: Asia Minor, Anatolia or Asiatic Turkey.

7   HYRCANIA: Area south-east of the Caspian Sea in Iran.

8   THRACIA: Thrace includes Eastern Greece, Turkey in Europe, and Southern Bulgaria.

9   GOSMAM: According to Kelly, 'Here appear great Hills, and veins of the Gold Mines appear: the men seem to have baskets of leather. This is one of the places under the Pole Artick.'

10   THEBAIDI: Thebes (Egypt) and surrounding area.

11   PARSADAL: Kelly, 'Here the sun shineth fair.' Most probably Pasargardae or Parsagarda ('the habitation of the Persians'), the ancient capital of Parsa/ Persis/ Persia Proper or the modern Iranian province of Fars (Part 74). Parsagarda is located about 60 miles north-east of Shiraz.

12   INDIA: Includes Indian provinces along the Indus River, roughly present-day Pakistan and India West of the Ganges (India Intra Ganges).

13   BACTRIANE: Bactriana covers Northern Afghanistan and the south-east of the Turkmen SSR, the River Amu-Dar'ya (Oxus) forming the northern boundary. For lands to the north of the river, see Sogdiana (Part 26).

14   CILICIA: Coastal country bordering the Mediterranean in south-east Turkey.

15   OXIANA: Alexandreia Oxiana, a town and its surrounding area on the Oxus River (Amu-Dar'ya) on the borders of Northern Afghanistan and the USSR.

16   NUMIDIA: Eastern Algerian coastal district between Africa (Part 86) and Mauretania (Part 91).

17   CYPRUS: Cyprus.

18   PARTHIA: North-east Iran, to the south of Hyrcania (Part 7). The region has a common border with the USSR.

19   GETULIA: The Western Sahara, south of Morocco, including Southern Algeria, Mali and the modern state of Mauritania.

20   ARABIA: Saudi Arabia.

21   PHALAGON: Dee: 'I have never heard of it.'
Kelly: 'It is toward the North, where the veines of Gold . . . appear . . . The men have things on their shoulders of beasts skins.'
Dee: 'Groynland as I think' (i.e. Greenland).

22   MANTIANA: This is Matiana or the Mattieni by Lacus Matianus (Lake Urmia) in Northern Iran. Lake Van, approximately 200 miles west in eastern Turkey, was once called Lake Mantiana.

23   SOXIA: Sacae/Sachia/Sakas approximates with Chinese Turkestan or Sinkiang in north-west China.
Kelly: 'People here appear of reddish colour.'

24   GALLIA: A 'greater' France with the Rhine forming the northern and eastern boundaries, thereby including Belgium, Luxemburg, and the Southern Netherlands.

25   ILLYRIA: At its greatest extent, Illyria included Central and Eastern Austria, Western Hungary or Transdanubia, Yugoslavia excluding Macedonia, Northern Bulgaria and Romania.

26   SOGDIANA: District between the Amu-Dar'ya (Oxus) and the Syr-Dar'ya (Jaxartes) rivers including the Uzbekistan SSR, with the cities of Bokhara and Samarkand, and Western Tadzhikistan SSR. Afghanistan is to the south, for which see Bactriana (Part 13).

27   LYDIA: Coastal region in Western Turkey.

28   CASPIS: Area to the south-west of the Caspian Sea in Iran.

29   GERMANIA: Includes modern Germany, Czechoslovakia and Poland and extends to the Italian border in the south, incorporating Switzerland and the Tyrol in Western Austria. In the north, Germania can include Denmark, Norway and Sweden, although Dee was told that Brytania (Part 61) could be used for Denmark, which at that time governed Norway as well.

30   TRENAM: Kelly: 'Here appear Monkies, great flocks. The people have leather Coats, and no beards, thick leather, and Garthers . . .'
Nalvage: 'These people are not known to you?'
Dee: 'Are they not in Africa?'
Nalvage: 'They be.'
Probably Teniam, a region on Jadocus Hondius's *World Map* (1608) straddling the Ivory Coast/Upper Volta/Ghana borderlands.

31   BITHYNIA: Black Sea coastal region in the north of Turkey, west of Paphlagonia (Part 40), including Istanbul (Asian side).

32   GRAECIA: Nalvage: 'A great Citie, and the Sea hard by it.'
Dee: 'Is not that great Citie Constantinople?'
Nalvage: 'It is . . .'
Graecia is thus Istanbul, not Greece; for which use Achaia (Part 37).

33   LICIA: Lycia is a country on the south coast of Turkey or Anatolia.

34   ONIGAP: Kelly: 'Here appear handsome men, in gathered tucked garments, and their shoes come up to the middle of their legs, of diverse coloured leather.'
Nalvage: 'These be beyond Hispaniola.'
Kelly: 'It is a low Countrey. Here appear great piles of Stones like St Andrews Crosses . . . There are on this side of it (a great way) a great number of dead Carkases . . .'
Nalvage: 'It is beyond Giapan.' (That is, beyond Japan across the Pacific to the Americas. Note that Onigap is an anagram of Giapon.)
Dee: 'Then it is that land, which I use to call Atlantis.'
Nalvage: 'They stretch more near the west.'
This can only be Mexico, particularly the Yucatan. Beyond Hispaniola (Haiti and Domenica) and west of 'Atlantis' or America is Central Mexico and the Yucatan, which is a low-lying peninsular. The people wore bright colours; the temples could resemble St Andrew's crosses; and, many people were slaughtered by the Spanish Conquistadores.

35   INDIA MAJOR: India Extra Gangem or India east of the Ganges, which includes all of South-East Asia.

36   ORCHENY: Nalvage: 'A great many little Isles.'
Dee: 'Do you mean the Isles of Orkney?' 'No.'
Dee: 'They seem to be the Isles of Malacha.'
Dee is mistakenly thinking of the islands around Malaya (Malacha or Malacca) or even the Moluccas. The Orcheni were a people south of

Chaldea (Part 72), living on or by islands in the marshlands of the lower Tigris and Euphrates.

37   ACHAIA: Southern Greece, including Athens and the Peloponnisos.

38   ARMENIA: Extensive region which, most comprehensively, stretches from the Euphrates in eastern Turkey to the Caspian Sea, thereby including Armenia SSR and the Azerbaijan SSR.

39   CILICIA (NEMROD): Nalvage: 'You never knew this Cilicia. This is Cilicia where the Children of Nemrod dwell. It is up in the Mountains beyond Cathay.'
This equates to the extreme north-eastern province of the USSR by the Bering Straits, the Magandanskaya Oblast. Cilicia in Turkey is Part 14.

40   PAPHLAGONIA: Black Sea çoastal country in the north of Turkey.

41   PHASIANA: District in Eastern Turkey, north of Lake Van, not to be confused with Phazania/Fezzan in Libya, for which see Garamantica (Part 45).

42   CHALDEI: The people of Chaldea (Part 72).

43   ITERGI: Nalvage: '. . . the people are yellow, tawney . . . They are to the south of the last Cilicians.' Possibly Mongolia, Manchuria (North-East China), and Korea.

44   MACEDONIA: Northern Greece and Southern Yugoslavia.

45   GARAMANTICA: Garamantes, a large area in Inner Africa, covering the Eastern Sahara, including the south of Libya (Fezzan), extreme south-eastern Algeria, Niger and Chad.

46   SAUROMATICA: Sarmatia or European Russia.

47   AETHIOPIA: Includes Ethiopia south of Egypt and also all of the unknown African continent south of the Equator, which was known as Ethiopia Interior in Dee's time. Unexplored parts of Africa north of the Equator were known as Libya Interior.

48   FIACIM: Kelly: 'Now he sheweth by the North Pole and the great Mountain.'
This is the North Pole. A great mountain was believed to exist at the Pole. See Map 6.

49   COLCHICA: Colchis is roughly the modern Russian state of Georgia, located to the east of the Black Sea.

50   CIRENIACA: Cyrenaica, a Mediterranean coastal region of Eastern Libya.

51   NASAMONIA: Ill-defined north-eastern Libyan coastal district by the Gulf of Sirte in the west of Cireniaca (Part 50).

52   CARTHAGO: Carthage, Tunisia.

53   COXLANT: Nalvage: 'It appeareth very Eastward.'
Kelly: 'It is on high ground. There come four Rivers out of it, one East, another West, another North, and another South . . . Is this the Paradise that Adam was banished out of?'
Nalvage: 'The very same.'
A discussion follows which does not help to locate Coxlant. The search for the Earthly Paradise, like the Eldorado, was the dream of early explorers. The four rivers are the Pison (The Persian Gulf?), Gihon (The Nile?), Hiddekel (Tigris), and Euphrates. The favourite location of Paradise was considered to be a little north of the confluence of the Tigris and Euphrates. However, other locations favoured sites further north in Mesopotamia and Armenia. Tibet could be another location. It is very easterly; on high ground; and the four rivers are the Mekong (east), the Indus (west), the Yangtze (north), and the Brahmaputra (south). Ultimately, however, the location of Coxlant or the Earthly Paradise must rest with the spirituality of the individual.

54   IDUMEA: Also called Edom, this is Southern Israel and Jordan.

55   PARSTAVIA: Actually Bastarnia, approximately Bessarabia or the Moldavia SSR to the east of Romania.

56   CELTICA: Nalvage: 'It is that which you call Flandria, the Low Country.'
This is North-West France and Belgium, not Central Gaul which is usually known as Celtica.

57   VINSAN: Kelly: 'Here appear men with tallons like Lions. They be very devils. There are five isles of them.'
    Suggest the ancient kingdom of Wu-Sun, south of Lake Balkhash in Kazakhstan, USSR. The 'isles' could be communities near the lake.

58   TOLPAM: Kelly: 'Under the South Pole.' This is Antarctica and Australasia.

59   CARCEDONIA: Carchedonia or modern Tunisia.

60   ITALIA: Italy, including the Istrian Peninsula in Yugoslavia.

61   BRYTANIA: The British Isles, Scandinavia, and places not included in the 91 parts.

62   PHENICES: Phoenicia, approximately the Lebanon and Northern Israel.

63   COMAGINEN: Commagene, a land-locked district in Southern Turkey, bounded on the east by the Euphrates and on the south by Syria. Cilicia (Part 14) is to the west.

64   APULIA: Province in south-east Italy between the Apennines and the Adriatic, bounded on the south by Calabria or the 'heel' of Italy.

65   MARMARICA: North African coastal region straddling the Egyptian and Libyan border. The Nile forms the eastern boundary.

66   CONCAVA SYRIA: Hollow Syria, usually known as Coele Syria, now forms Northern Syria.

67   GEBAL: Later Byblos, now Jubail, about twenty miles north of Beirut.

68   ELAM: Also known as Susiana, it is approximately the same as the modern Iranian province of Khuzestan at the north of the Persian Gulf, bordering Iraq and including Abadan.

69   IDUNIA: Nalvage: 'It is beyond Greenland.'

70   MEDIA: North-Western Iran, south of Caspis (Part 28) and Hyrcania (Part 7). Includes Teheran.

71   ARIANA: Eastern Iran, Pakistan west of the Indus, Southern Afghanistan.

72   CHALDEA: A tract of country in South Iraq running along the Euphrates from the Persian Gulf to Babylon (about 50 miles south of Bagdad). The Shamiya Desert forms the western boundary.

73   SERICIPOPULI: A people in Eastern Asia. Serica or Seres equates with China and the Far East.

74   PERSIA: Persis or Parsa, this is approximately the modern Iranian province of Fars. Located in south-west Iran and bounded on the west by the Persian Gulf, the province was the kernel of ancient Persia and includes the ancient cities of Parsagarda (Part 11) and Persepolis.

75   GONGATHA: Kelly: 'Towards the South Pole.'

This is Gongala, an area to the south of Libya Interior by the Equator. In the sixteenth century Kelly's description is apt, but today the region equates with South Sudan.

76   GORSIM: Kelly: 'Beares and Lions here.'
Most probably Korasim/Chorasim/Gerazi an ancient site at the north of Lake Tiberias (Sea of Galilee), Israel. Note also the Chorasmii south-east of the Caspian Sea in modern Turkmen SSR.

77   HISPANIA: Spain and Portugal.

78   PAMPHILIA: Southern Turkish coastal land, between Lycia (Part 33) and Cilicia (Part 14), forming a narrow strip of land around the Bay of Antalya.

79   OACIDI: This is Oasitae (' . . . of the Oasis'), the oasis area west of the Nile, which includes the great oasis of the Oracle of Amon.

80   BABYLON or BABYLONIA: Region in Southern Iraq, extending north from the Persian Gulf between the Lower Tigris and the north-eastern Arabian desert. Babylon, the capital, is about fifty miles south of Bagdad.

81   MEDIAN: Kelly: 'It is much Northward.'
Note, however, Midian – the land of the Midianites by Sinai; or, even the people of Media (Part 70).

82   IDUMIAN: Kelly: 'They are two Isles environed with an arm of the Scythian Sea, which goeth in at Maspi.'
Most probably the region to the north-east of the Aral Sea in the Kazakhstan SSR. Suggest 'Maspi' is a corruption of the Aspisii Montes / Mons Aspisii, which shortened to M. Aspisii, distorts to Maspi. The mountains were supposedly located in this region, but in the sixteenth century much of this land and especially the far north of Siberia or Scythia was Terrae Incognita. Mercator's map of North-East Asia, which is dated 1569, shows a hypothetical arm of the Scythian Sea (Laptev and East Siberian seas) almost reaching to the north-east of the Aral Sea with the M. Aspisii nearby. The Aspisii Scythea were the people dwelling to the west of the mountains and to the north of the River Jaxartes (Syr-Dar'ya). Note also, however, the Arimaspi detailed in Part 88 below. The Maspii, a noble Persian tribe, are too far south to be considered.

83   FELIX ARABIA: Arabian Red Sea coastlands, particularly the south-western areas, including the Yemen.

84   METAGONITIDIM: The Metagonitae were a people living in Tangiers and the surrounding area. The district forms the west of Mauretania (Part 91) or modern Northern Morocco.

85   ASSYRIA: Eastern Iraq between the Tigris and the Iranian border.

86   AFRICA: Mediterranean coastal region of Libya, including Tripoli and the modern province of Tripolitania, but excluding the eastern part, for which see Cireniaca (Part 50) and Nasamonia (Part 51). The region also includes the eastern Algerian coastlands and the Algerian/Tunisian border. This is not the continent of Africa.

87   BACTRIANI: The people of Bactriana (Part 13).

88   AFNAN or AFRAN: Kelly: 'Here appear people with one eye in their head, seeming to be in their breast, towards the Equinoctial.'
Dee: 'I remember of people called Arimaspi.'
Dee is confused here, as the Arimaspi ('the one-eyed') were a people on the left bank of the Middle Volga, north of the Caspian Sea. The Afran are the people Ptolemy called the Aphricerones, located just north of Equatorial Africa in North Zaire. The ancient scholars considered that all the southern parts of Africa were uninhabitable (as with many unexplored lands) and populated with strange beasts. Herodotus included in his conjectures on unknown Africa descriptions of peoples with 'one eye in the breast instead of the usual head', which must be the people referred to.

89   PHRYGIA: Large province in Central Turkey. Greater Phrygia was bounded on the east by Cappadocia (Part 4).

90   CRETA: Crete.

91   MAURITANIA or MAURETANIA: Morocco and the north Algerian coastlands, not to be confused with the modern state of Mauritania, which is located further south and for which see Getulia (Part 19).

Notes

1   Henry Cornelius Agrippa. *Occult Philosophy*. 1533.
2   Meric Casaubon. *A True & Faithful Relation of what passed for many Years between Dr. John Dee . . . and some Spirits*, London, 1659, p. 153; and pp. 153–159 for all quotations following.
3   Dee, like most of his contemporaries, believed the island of Friseland to exist. It was, in fact, a duplication of Iceland on an early map (see Map 6), an error which was repeated. When its coast was supposedly skirted, this was actually the coast of Cape Farewell, Southern Greenland. Note also that today Germania (Part 29) incorporates Poland. In Dee's time Poland was located much further eastward and would have formed part of Sarmatia or Russia (Part 46).

References

Geography of Claudius Ptolemy, New York, 1932.
Kiepert, H., *Formae Orbis Antiqua*, Berlin, 1894.
Louis, V. de St Martin, *Atlas dressé pour l'histoire de la geographie et des decouvertes geographiques*, Paris, 1874.
Oestergaards Handatlas, Berlin, 193–.
Skelton, R. A., *Decorative and Printed Maps of the Fifteenth to Eighteenth Centuries*, London, 1965.
Smith, W., *Dictionary of Greek and Roman Geography*, London, 1878.
Taylor, E. G. R., *Tudor Geography: 1485–1583*, London, 1930.

Appendix D
Guide to the Maps

Maps 1 to 4 give the 91 parts of the physical world and their corresponding numbers, as detailed in Sloane MS. 3191. The usual form of the name (if any) is given beneath in square brackets, e.g.

SAUROMATICA
[SARMATIA]

Duplicated names in round brackets indicate possible alternative locations, e.g.

(COXLANT 53)

All boundaries are given where possible. Unnamed bounded areas are lands which are not included in the 91 parts and are only included to show the extent of an adjacent listed area. Named but unnumbered areas, e.g. Scythia, are included to ease location of lands.

Provincial boundaries within major areas are indicated by a slightly lighter line.

Maps 5 to 7 are adaptations of sixteenth-century maps (listed below). From these it can be seen that a considerable Arctic land mass was believed to exist; hence the North Polar locations indicated at the top of Map 4. The Antarctic coastline shown as part of TOLPAM (58) is not inaccurate.

Map 5 is a sixteenth-century map of the world based upon THEATRUM ORBIS TERRARUM by Ortelius (1570).

Map 6 is based upon a map published in 1595 and shows the northern polar region as Gerhard Mercator imagined it to be.

Map 7 shows the southern polar region, based upon a map from SPECULUM ORBIS TERRAE by Gerard and Cornelius de Jode (1593).

Map 8 shows the world according to Ptolemy, *c.* AD 150.

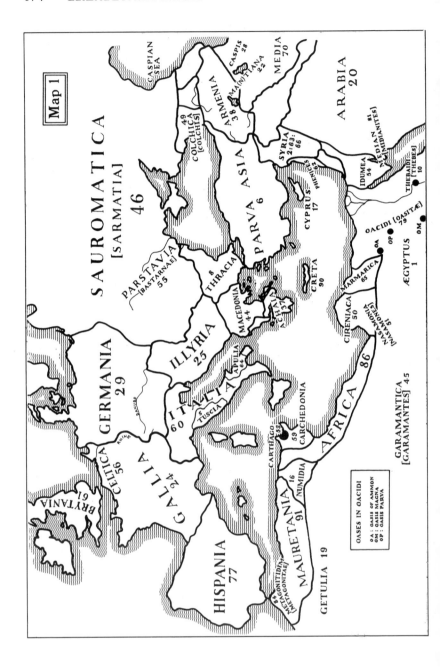

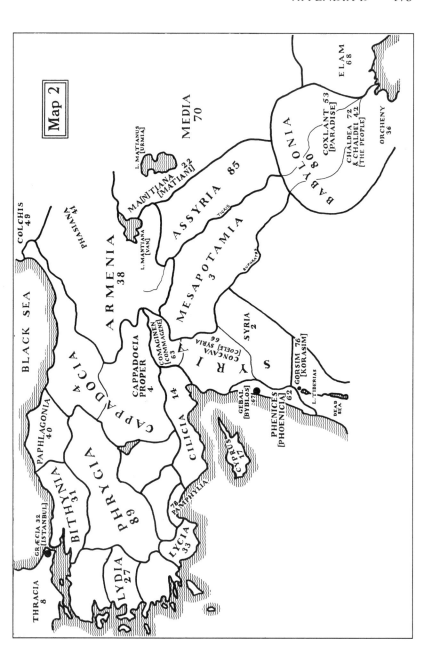

Map 2

Map 3

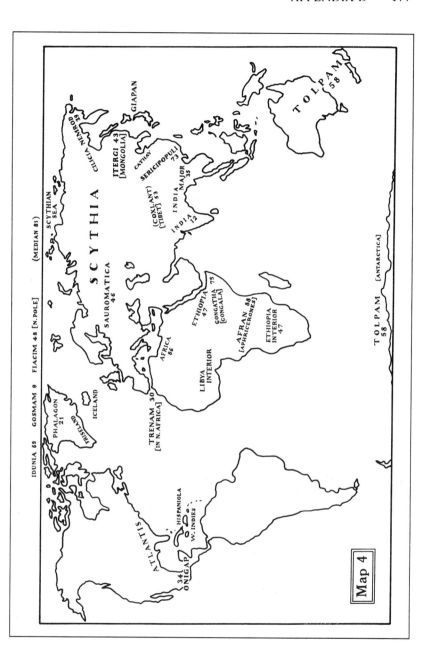

Map 4

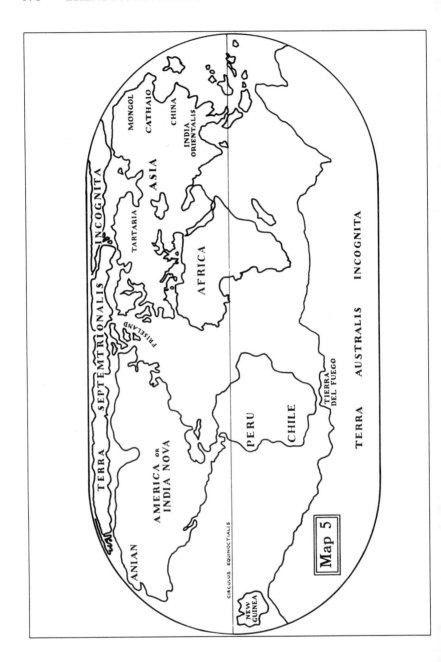

Map 5

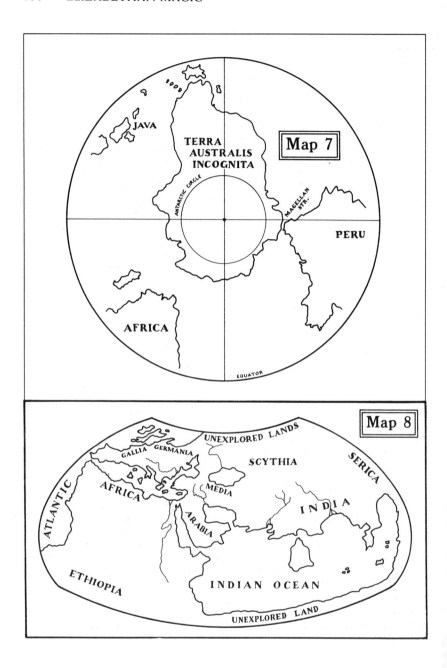

Bibliography

John Dee

Manuscripts (British Library)

Sloane MS. 3188, *Libri Mysteriorū* I–V in Dee's hand.
Sloane MS. 3677, Elias Ashmole's transcription of Sloane 3188.
Sloane MS. 3191, Dee's four books of Angelic magic in his own hand.
Sloane MS. 3678, Elias Ashmole's transcription of Sloane 3191.
Sloane MS. 3189, *The Book of Enoch, or Liber Logaeth* in Edward Kelly's hand.
Additional MS. 36674, Magical Treatise by Caius, Forman, Dee and Kelly.

Printed Works

Agrippa, Henry Cornelius, *Three Books of Occult Philosophy*, Chthonios Books, 1987.
Casaubon, Meric (ed.), *A True and Faithful Relation of what passed for many Yeers Between Dr John Dee . . . and some Spirits*, London, 1659 (reprinted Askin, 1974).
Deacon, Richard, *John Dee – Scientist, Geographer, Astrologer and Secret Agent to Elizabeth I*, London, 1968.
Dee, John, *The Hieroglyphic Monad*, tr. J. W. Hamilton Jones, London, 1947.
French, Peter J., *John Dee – The World of an Elizabethan Magus*, Routledge & Kegan Paul, London, 1972.
Halliwell, James O. (ed.), *The Private Diary of Dr John Dee*, Camden Society, London, 1842.
James, G. (ed. and tr.), *The Enochian Evocation of Dr John Dee*, Heptangle Books & Gillette, New Jersey, 1984.
Laycock, D. C., *The Complete Enochian Dictionary*, Askin, London, 1978.
Leasor, James, *The Plague and the Fire*, Pan Books, 1966.
Ronan, Colin A., *Their Majesties Astronomers*, Bodley Head, London, 1967.
Schueler, Gerald J., *Enochian Magic – A Practical Manual* and *Enochian Magick – An Advanced Guide*, Llewellyn, 1987.
Smith, Thomas, *The Life of John Dee*, tr. William A. Ayton, London, 1908.
Suster, Gerald, *John Dee – Essential Readings*, Crucible, 1986.
Tait, Fiona, and Upton, Christopher (tr.), *The Steganographia of Johannes Trithemius*, Magnum Opus Hermetic Sourceworks, Edinburgh, 1982.
Taylor, E. G. R., *Tudor Geography (1485–1583)*, Octagon Books, New York, 1968.
Turner, Robert (ed.), *The Heptarchia Mystica of John Dee*, Aquarian Press, Wellingborough, 1986.
Walker, D. P., *Spiritual and Demonic Magic – from Ficino to Campanella*, London, 1975.
Williams, Gwyn A., *Welsh Wizard and British Empire*, University College, Cardiff, 1980.

Additional Sources

Clulee, N. H., *At the Crossroads of Magic and Science: John Dee's Archemastrie*, Cambridge University Press, 1984.

Ford, Boris (ed.), *The Age of Shakespeare*, Pelican Books, 1962.
Josten, C. H., 'An Unknown Chapter in the Life of John Dee', *Journal of the Warburg and Courtauld Institutes*, Vol. 28, London, 1965.
McCulloch, Samuel Clyde, 'John Dee: Elizabethan Doctor of Science and Magic', *The South Atlantic Quarterly*.
'Queen Elizabeth's Astrologer – Notes on the Diary of Dr John Dee', *The Month*, Vol. 158, 1931.

Simon Forman

Manuscripts

Additional MS. 36674, contains a magical text in Forman's hand.
Sloane MS. 3702, *Operation by the Regal Spirit Usiel.*

Printed Works

Halliwell, James O. (ed.), *The Diaries of Simon Forman*, London, 1843 (Proof copy for consideration for publication by the Camden Society, but abandoned owing to some objectionable paragraphs), British Library. Other copies were privately printed in 1849 and 1853.
Hole, Christina, *Witchcraft in England*, Charles Scribner's Sons, London, 1947.
Johnson, Paul, *Elizabeth I*, Omega, Futura Publications, London, 1976.
Rowse, A. L., *The Case Books of Simon Forman*, Picador, London, 1976.

Robert Fludd

Godwin, Joscelyn, *Robert Fludd – Hermetic Philosopher and Surveyor of Two Worlds*, Thames & Hudson, London, 1979.
Hall, Manly P., *The Adepts in the Western Esoteric Tradition*, Los Angeles, 1949.
_____ *The Secret Teachings of All Ages*, Los Angeles, 1962.
Holy Cross Church Bearsted – a Short Account (guide book), Anon, 1972.
Jacobi, Jolanda (ed.), *Paracelsus – Selected Writings*, Pantheon Books, New York, 1958.
Josten, C. H., 'Robert Fludd's Theory of Geomancy', *Journal of the Warburg and Courtauld Institutes*, Vol. 27, London, 1964.
Rowse, A. L., *The Elizabethan Renaissance*, Sphere Books, London, 1974 (Cardinal).
Skinner, Stephen, *Terrestrial Astrology – Divination by Geomancy*, Routledge & Kegan Paul, London, 1980.
Waite, A. E., *The Brotherhood of the Rosy Cross*, University Books, New York.
Wilson, Colin, *Mysteries*, Hodder & Stoughton, London, 1978.
Yates, Frances A., *The Rosicrucian Enlightenment*, Paladin, 1975.
_____ *The Occult Philosophy in the Elizabethan Age*, Ark, 1983.

Thomas Jones of Tregaron

Printed Works

Barber, Chris, *Mysterious Wales*, Paladin, Granada Publishing, 1983.
Calendar of State Papers, Domestic Series, James I, 1611–18, Vol. LXIX, p. 130. Letters and Papers, numbers 11–15 (Undated).

The Cambro-Britain and General Celtic Repository, 1819–22, Vol. I, p. 212.

Davies, R. Isgarn, *Thomas Jones (Twm Shon Catti), Porth y ffynon, Bard, Genealogist, Antiquary and Gentleman, 1530–1609*. (D. C. Rees: *The History of Tregaron*. 1936)

Deacon, W. F., *Twm John Catty: The Welch Rob Roy* (The Innkeeper's Album, London, 1823) Fiction/Folklore.

Dictionary of National Biography (Microprint Version).

Dodd, A. H., *Life in Wales*, Chapter IV, Batsford, 1972.

——— *A Short History of Wales*, Chapter IV, Batsford, Sixth Impression, 1987.

Exchequer Proceedings James I: Thos. Jones alias "Twm Shon Catti" 12 February 1609/10, at the town of Caron, p. 563 (tr. Carm. Antiq. Soc. and Field Club, Vol. 29).

Hughes, Lynn, *Hawkmoor, Adventures of Twm Sion Cati*, Christopher Davies/ Penguin, 1977.

Jones, J. Frederick, *Thomas Jones of Tregaron alias Twm Shon Catti (1530–1609)*.

The Life, Exploits, and Death of Twm John Catty, 1830 (A sixpenny Romance).

Meyrick, S. R., *History of Cardiganshire*, 1810, pp. 247–51.

——— (ed.), *Lewys Dwnn: Heraldic Visitations of Wales between 1586 and 1613*, Llandovery, 1846, pp. 7, 45, 46 constituting Meyrick's notes to Dwnn's sixteenth-century Welsh text.

Myfrian Archaiology of Wales, collected out of ancient MSS, by Owen Jones, 1801–7.

Nicholas, Thomas, *Annals and Antiquities of the Counties and County Families of Wales*, 1872, Vol. I, pp. 272–3.

Owen, G. Dyfnallt, *Elizabethan Wales*, University of Wales Press, Reprint 1986.

Prichard, T. J. L., *The Adventures and Vagaries of Twm Shon Catti*, 3rd edn, Llanielloes, 1873 (Fiction). *Poem: Cywdd y Govid: 'Poem of Affliction'* tr. Iolo Morganwg in text.

Roberts, Prof. Glyn, *Aspects of Welsh History*, University of Wales Press, 1969.

Thomas, Sir Rhys ap, *The Blood of the Raven by Francis Jones*. (Transactions of the Carmarthenshire Antiquarian Society and Field Club, Vol. 29, 1938/9.)

Transactions of the Carmarthenshire Antiquarian Society and Field Club, Vol. 9, 1913, p. 16.

Tregaron WI, *Tregaron. The WI looks around its Town & Country*, Tregaron WI, 1984.

Magazines

Welsh Gazette, 24 and 31 May 1928. Copy of a *Bill of Complaint* with spelling 'modernised'.

Western Mail, 17 Aug. 1938. An excerpt from a report by J. Kyle Fletcher on 'City's Treasury of Old Welsh Books'; it includes a reference to Twm's work as a genealogist.

Western Mail, 4 Aug. 1973. Lynn Hughes, *The Humorous Exploits of the Welsh Robin Hood. Is Twm the real Tom Jones?*

Additional Sources

B. M. *The Myfrian Archaiology, 1870*.

B. M. Cotton Charter XIII. art. 38.

B. M. Cotton Charter XIV. art. 1.

B. M. Harleian MS. 5835. art. 2.

B. M. Harleian MS. 473.

The Concise Oxford Dictionary (5th edn, 1976).

The Compendious Rehearsal of John Dee his Dutiful Declaration and Proofe of the Course and Race of his Studious Life, for the Space of Halfe an Hundred Years, now (by God's Favour and help) Fully Spent, and of the Very Great Injuries, Damages and Indignities Which for These Last Nine Years he Hath in England Sustained . . . Made unto the Two Honourable Commissioners, by Her Most Excellent Majestie Thereto Assigned, 1592. (Original in B. M. Cotton MS; Vitell. C. vii, 1. Printed by T. Hearne in the appendix to *Johannes Glastoniensis Chronicon*.)

Gwarg-gower Dictionary.

Halliwell, James O. (ed.), *The Private Diary of Dr John Dee*, Camden Society, London, 1842.

Johnson, Paul, *Elizabeth I*, Omega, Futura Publications, 1976.

The New Collins Spurrell Welsh Dictionary, 1960.

Oxford. Ashmole MS. 847. fols.1^v and 118^v.

Reid, William, *Arms Through The Ages*, A. B. Nordbok, Gothenburg, Sweden, 1976.

Rhys, Sir John, *Celtic Folklore*, Vol. 2, Wildwood House, London, 1980.

Thomson, Derick S. (ed.), *The Companion to Gaelic Scotland*, Basil Blackwell, 1983.

Turner, Robert (ed.), *The Heptarchia Mystica of John Dee*, Aquarian Press, 1986.

Robert Turner of 'Holshott': Published Works

Original Writings

[BOTANOLOGIA] BOTANOΛOΓIA. The Brittish Physician: or, The Nature and Vertues of English Plants, London, 1664.

[BOTANOLOGIA], London, 1687. Reprint of 1664 edition with portrait.

[MIKROKOSMOS] *MIKPOKOΣMOΣ. A Description of the Little-World, being a discovery of the Body of Man exactly delineating all the members, bones, veins sinews, arteries, and parts thereof, from the head to the foot. Hereunto is added . . . the cure of wounds . . . the sicknesses attributed to the twelve Signes and Planets, with their Natures, London, 1654.*

Woman's Counsellor, or the Feminine Physician, modestly treating of such occult accidents and secret diseases incident to that sex, London [1657?]. Sold by Nathaniel Brook at the Angel in Cornhill.

Woman's Counsellor, or the Feminine Physician, London, 1686. Reprint of first edition.

Translations

Arbatel of Magick, De Magia Veterum, 1655. Bound with the *Fourth Book*.

Arbatel of Magick, 2nd edn, Gillette, New Jersey, 1979.

Archidoxes of Magic, by Paracelsus, London, 1975. 2nd edn of *Of the Supreme Mysteries of Nature*.

Ars Notoria: The Notary Art of Solomon; shewing the Cabalistic key of magical operations, the liberal sciences, divine revelation, and the art of memory. Whereunto is added an Astrological Catechism, fully demonstrating the art of Judicial Astrology. Written originally in Latine by Apollonius, Leovitius and others, and now Englished by R. Turner. London, 1657.

Ars Notoria: The Notary Art of Solomon. 2nd edn Seattle, Washington, 1987. Omits Turner's introduction of 1657.

An Astrological Catechisme, wherein the Art of Judicial Astrology is fully demonstrated by way of Q. and A. Tr. out of Leovitius and revised by Robert Turner, 1657. Bound with the *Ars Notoria*.

Astrologicall Opticks. Wherein are represented the Faces of every Signe, with the Images of each Degree in the Zodiack; by Johannes Angelus [Johann Engel]. London, 1655.

Astronomical Geomancy; by Gerard of Cremona, 1655. Bound with the *Fourth Book*.

Compleat Bone-Setter: Being the Method of Curing Broken Bones, Dislocated Joynts, and Ruptures, commonly called Broken Bellies. Written originally by Friar [Thomas] Moulton; Englished and enlarged by Robert Turner. London, 1656.

Compleat Bone-Setter. 2nd edn, London, 1665. Includes portrait which was redrawn for the 1687 reprint of the *Botanologia*.

Compleat Bone-Setter. Isleworth, Middlesex: Tamor Pierston, 1981. Forty-eight-page facsimile of parts of the 1656 edition.

Enchiridion Medicum: An Enchiridion of the Art of Physick Methodically prescribing Remedies . . . to the Sick-Man . . . Containing a salubrious remedy for every malady incident to the body of Man. Written in Latin by our learned countryman John Sadler, Doctor in Physick; tr. revised, corrected and augmented by R. Turner. London, 1657.

Fourth Book of Occult Philosophy; attributed to Henry Cornelius Agrippa. London, 1655.

Fourth Book of Occult Philosophy, 2nd edn, London, 1978.

Heptameron: or, Magical Elements; ascribed to Peter de Abano. 1655. Bound with the *Fourth Book*.

Isagoge . . . Of the Nature of Spirits; by Georg Pictorius von Villingen, 1655. Bound with the *Fourth Book*.

Of the Chymical Transmutation, Genealogy, and Generation of Metals and Minerals, by Paracelsus, London, 1657.

Of Geomancy; attributed to Henry Cornelius Agrippa, 1655. Bound with the *Fourth Book*.

Of the Supreme Mysteries of Nature, by Paracelsus. Englished by R. Turner, London, 1656.

Philosophical and Chymical Experiments of that famous Philosopher Raymond Lully; containing the right and due Composition of both Elixirs; the admirable and perfect way of making the great Stone of the Philosophers . . . Now for the benefit of all lovers of Art and Knowledge, carefully translated out of High German and Latin, by W. W., student in the Celestial Sciences, and R. T. 1657. Bound with *Of the Chymical Transmutation*.

Sal, Lumen et Spiritus Mundi Philosophici: or, the dawning of the Day, discovered by the beams of light; shewing, the true salt and secrets of the philosophers, the first and universal Spirit of the World. Written originally in French by Clovis Hesteau, Sieur de Nuysement and afterwards turned into Latin by the illustrious Doctor Lodovicus Combachius [Ludwig Combach] and now transplanted into Albyons Garden by R. T. London, 1657.

Edward Kelly

The Alchemical Writings of Edward Kelly (Preface by A. E. Waite), Stuart & Watkins, London, 1970.

Wilson, Colin, *The Occult*, Mayflower Books, 1973.

Dee's private diary and various manuscripts.

Index